The Nondescript God

"Abstraction or Paragon?"

M. K. Sudarshan

© M K Sudarshan 2022

All rights reserved

All rights reserved by author. No part of this publication may be reproduced, stored in a retrieval system or transmitted in any form or by any means, electronic, mechanical, photocopying, recording or otherwise, without the prior permission of the author.

Although every precaution has been taken to verify the accuracy of the information contained herein, the author and publisher assume no responsibility for any errors or omissions. No liability is assumed for damages that may result from the use of information contained within.

First Published in April 2022

ISBN: 978-93-5611-235-3

BLUEROSE PUBLISHERS

www.bluerosepublishers.com
info@bluerosepublishers.com
+91 8882 898 898

Cover Design:
Muskan Sachdeva

Typographic Design:
Pooja Sharma

Distributed by: BlueRose, Amazon, Flipkart

This Book has been graced by the SRI AHOBILA MUTT *lineage of Acharyas of recent past and present.*

|| "Sri Mukham" ||

From
SRI KARYAM
SRI AHOBILA MATH
ஸ்ரீ அஹோபில மடம்

HH 46th Jeer

        According to Hindu orthodox systems the sruti-s (Veda-s) , more specifically , the Upaniashad-s are the ultimate source of valid authority for knowing the true nature of the Supreme Reality- the Brahman. These sacred scriptures in its entirety glorify the cause of the Universe- the Supreme Brahman, says, Acharya Sri Ramanuja thus : अस्य वैभव प्रतिपादनपरा: श्रुतय: (Vide: Vedartha Sangraha). Not only Sri Ramanuja but also almost all other preceptors , more or less , are of the same view. The Upanishad-s are many and, the various statements of the Upanisha-s appear to be contradictory in nature when they speak about Brahman, at least at the surface level. An in-depth study of these seemingly contradictory passages would make it clear that there is no contradiction in the views of the Upanishad-s. Thus, when they declare Brahman as devoid of attributes in a specific sense and in a particular context and, as endowed with many other noble attributes it is to be understood that Brahman is devoid of the imperfect qualities and when they speak Brahman as associated with attributes , it is to be taken as endowed with noble qualities. This is the twin aspect of Brahman, namely, Ubhayalingatva (उभयलिङ्गत्व) according to the tradition of Sri Ramanuja.

        In the modern context not many are aware of the true significance and interpretation of these Saguna and Nirguna passages of these Upanishad-s and, the present book of Sri M.K. Sudarsan is a wonderful attempt in this direction. The author, Sri M.K Sudarsan has followed the interpretations of the Visishtadvaita preceptors in this regard. He drew inspiration, particularly, from the commentary on Sri Vishnu Sahasranama of Sri Parasarabhatta, the Bhagavd-guna-darpana.

P. T. O

The contents of the book were well looked into and explained to HH Srimad Azhagiyasingar, the 46th Pontiff of Sri Ahobila Math. HH Srimad Azhagiyasingar feels very happy for the efforts of Sri M.K Sudarsan and felt that many more such publications must be brought to propagate the upanishadic philosophy. He blessed Sri M.K.Sudarsan for his efforts and wished him all success in his future endeavors.

By the order of HH the Jeer of Sri Ahobila Math

Camp : Coimbatore

Date : 27th February 2022

Dr. Padmanabhacharyar
SRIKARYAM
PRINCIPAL SECRETARY TO
HIS HOLINESS THE 46th JEER
OF SRI AHOBILA MUTT.

|| *"Sri:"* ||

HH Sri Ranganatha Yatindra Mahadesikan
46th Azhagiyasingar - present Acharya of Sri Ahobila Mutt

The Nondescript God

"Abstraction or Paragon?"

Dialogues on *"Nirguna Brahman"*
with
"An Unknown Sri Vaishnava"

A VISISHTAADVAITA PERSPECTIVE

Based on **SRI VEDANTA DESIKA'S** *"satadushani" and* **SRI PARASHARA BHATTAR'S** *commentary, the "bhagavath guna darpana" on the* **"Sri Vishnu Sahasranaama"**

M.K. SUDARSHAN

Preface

At a time when both authors and readers of serious topics are rather scarce, **Sri M.K. Sudarshan** has chosen a subject of substantial significance to discourse on. In the humdrum of our daily lives, misplaced priorities are the order of the day and the time devoted to spiritual thought and practice has dwindled to five or ten minutes in the morning before we rush off to our "more productive" endeavours. Further, the attention span of the modern reader has shrunk to such an extent that he prefers "capsules" and snippets, rather than read with patience a few full pages of text, however profound they are. Days are such that if Sri Krishna were to revisit us, the "busy" reader would perhaps ask Him to condense the **Bhagavath Gita** to a single page.

However, there is a difference between the ordinary author whose intentions are commercial and who hankers after his five minutes of fame and the serious author who is prompted by the desire to learn and to pass on to posterity the lamp of enlightenment which he received from his preceptor. The latter is more gratified if his words strike a chord in the heart of even a few of his readers who are prompted to embark on a journey of seeking in the spiritual realm. Hence, we can understand the motive behind **Sri Sudarshan's** present endeavour.

Another modern thought is that we should emphasize harmony and not dwell on divisions, be they spiritual, philosophical, social or economic. Whether it is the difference between *Smarthas* and *Vaishnavas*, *Advaitis*, *Dvaitis* and *Visishtadvaitis* or between religions, we are supposed to ignore them and adopt a common denominator, which ultimately results in no one following the path trodden well by their forebears. Little do people realise that religions and philosophies *will* have differences and the wise man doesn't ignore them but is tolerant towards tenets different from his own. People remember only too well what happened to Emperor Akbar's *Din Ilahi*. What people need is faith in their religions while not looking down or up at others'. *Vanangum turaigal pala pala aakki* says **Sri Nammazhwar** and *Naatinaan deivam engum nallador arul tannaale* says **Sri Tondaradippodi**, emphasising that the plurality in all the above is part of the good Lord's Creation. Hence, while what **Sri Sudarshan** has set out to do may not win him the hearts of the modern-day 'secularists', it is nonetheless essential. The honest author must always remember that he is not running for a popularity contest by penning what people want to read most, but to tell the truth, as he sees it, whether or not it is palatable to the proletariat, adhering to the credo of **Sri Nammazhwar** of calling a spade a spade, whether or not it endears him to most (*sonnaal virodham idu, aagilum solluvan kenmino*).

The question **Sri Sudarshan** has attempted to address is, so to say, as old as the hills. Contrary to popular misconception, *Visishtadvaitis* had differences with *Advaitis* much before **Sri Ramanuja**, who, in the prologue to his commentary on the *Brahma Sutras*, says he is toeing the path of his predecessors like **Tanka, Dramidacharya, Guhadeva, Kapardi, Baruchi**, *et al*. With our *Purvaachaaryas*, it was not a question of engaging in polemics for displaying their erudition but emphasising that the glorious *Brahman* should not be reduced to the status of a colourless, odourless, formless, shapeless and inert substance, much like a gaseous element. They were keen to assert, based on the *Shruti*, that the Supreme *Brahman* is an ocean of auspicious attributes with none equal to or higher in glory, beauty or magnificence (*yasmaat param naaparam asti kinchit*). The so-called sectarian differences did not however degenerate to name-calling or derogatory references, as they are wont to nowadays. Healthy philosophical differences and debates have been an integral part of *Sanatana Dharma*, to which the **Brahma Sutras** stand as eloquent testimony. There have never been attempts at papering over differences and presenting a false façade of hypocritical unity.

Now, one would imagine that all that needs to be said on the subject has already been said and eloquently too. Both *Advaitis* and *Visishtadvaitis* have been prolific in authoring works upholding their own tenets and decrying that of others. Where then is the need for one more book on the subject? Is it not *pishta peshanam* or grinding the flour repeatedly? Yes, it is indeed true that there is almost nothing left unsaid in the matter. However, all that exists is arguments and counterarguments between scholars, couched in a highfalutin language comprehensible only to them, that too in chaste **Sanskrit** or **Manipravalam**, both of which are beyond the reach of the modern reader, who is barely conversant with his mother tongue, but proficient in the international *lingua franca*, English. It is to cater to this segment of readers, who are serious enough about philosophy to ask questions and would like to embark on a journey of spiritual inquiry, but for being handicapped by the non-availability of books that clearly and honestly deal with this thorny issue in a comprehensible style, without resorting to bewildering jargon and a display of erudition that is of little benefit to the reader. This, then, is the laudable objective of this book.

The two great works **Sri Sudarshan** has based his monograph upon, the *Satadushani* of **Swami Vedanta Desika** and the *Bhagavad Guna Darpanam* of **Swami Parasara Bhattar,** are acclaimed works of the **Sri Vaishnava** tenet. The former is a transcript of the debate Swami Desikan had with *Advaitis* in Srirangam and is considered a seminal work incorporating the arguments of *Purvaachaaryas* and developing on them. Unfortunately, only 66 of the original 100 arguments are extant, but what is available is quite adequate to serve the author's intended purpose. *Satadushani*'s importance can be gauged by philosopher and Sanskrit scholar **Sri Surendranath**

Dasgupta devoting no less than 40 pages to this particular work, in his *History of Indian Philosophy*. The English introduction of **Sri R. Kesava Iyengar** to the commentary of **Mahavidvan Chetlur Srivatsankacharya Swami** on *Satadushani* is indeed excellent and exhaustive.

And the *Bhagavad Guna Darpanam* is the only commentary on **Sri Vishnu Sahasranama Stotra** to adopt an innovative, thematic approach to the thousand glorious names of the Lord. Each of these wonderful sobriquets represents a particular attribute (*yaani naamaani gounaani*), thus denying *prima facie* the notion of a *nirguna Brahman*.

Having such strong guide rails as the *Bhagavad Guna Darpanam* and the *Satadushani* is a great advantage of **Sri Sudarshan's** work and helps him stay focussed on the issue, bringing out the nuggets embedded in both and offering them in an easy-to-understand format.

It is always an object of wonderment for the uninitiated as to how two scholars of renown could differ about the essential nature of *Brahman*, its relationship with its adjuncts --- the sentients and the non-sentients --- what salvation represents, etc. And differ so much as to offer diametrically opposite interpretations to many of the *Upanishadic* texts which are straightforward! However, as **Sri Alavandar** says, even giant intellects can fall prey to delusion, leading to the perception of existing things as non-existent and *vice versa*. One man's food could be another man's poison, we hear; however, here is a case of *Visishtadvaitis* regarding the *Advaitis* as those with skewed perception (*kudrishtis*) and the latter returning the 'compliment' to the former in stronger terms, all based on the same *Veda vaakyas* both swear by. Answers to these and other questions are to be found in the following pages, answers that shed light, provoke curiosity and the desire for further exploration and are couched in a logical, coherent, and smooth-flowing narrative.

Presenting in English the complex concepts of philosophy, especially those advanced by the *Satadushani*, is no easy task. And to present them in good, readable English bereft of jargon is still more difficult. The author has succeeded in doing these in good measure. **Sri Sudarshan** has a way with words, making them dance to the lilting tunes he sets, intended and unintended alliterations serving as an adornment to the text.

It is indeed presumptuous of me to write this much when the venerable *Sri Karyam Swami* of **Sri Ahobila Mutt** has already adorned this work with his *Sri Mukham* above and has said all there is to say. Still, this is my two pennies' worth, as they say.

K. Sadagopa Iyengar
Editor, "*Sri Nrisimha Priya*"
Journal of the Sri Ahobila Mutt

28.2.2022

Prologue

After the three editions of my book, **"The Unusual Essays of an Unknown Sri Vaishnava"** (see Page 119) were published (in **2016, 2018, and 2021**), many readers -- after having gained from its reading a greater awareness of Sri Vaishnavism than ever before, and of its ancient philosophy, vast scriptural literature in Sanskrit and Tamizh and of its many diverse religious practices and traditions -- wrote to me expressing curiosity in knowing more about the main differences between **Advaita** and **Visishtaadvaita** metaphysics.

The most fundamental difference between the tenets of Advaita and Visisishtaadvaita schools of Vedanta philosophy is their respective conception of Theism --- i.e. of one supreme Godhead and Creator known as *Brahman* in the Vedic **Upanishads**.

Advaita posits Brahman as a formless, attribute-less, **nondescript**, ontological gnostic entity called **"Nirgunan"** or Pure Consciousness. Visishtaadvaita affirms its conception of Brahman to be **"Sagunan,"** a God who is a **paragon** of infinitely auspicious qualities and wondrous perfections. It however does not deny Brahman to be *"nirguna"* too but interprets that quality uniquely in accordance with and on the authority of the Vedanta Sutra.

The two schools base their positions on their respective interpretation of the ageless Vedic scriptures called **"sruti"** and **"smriti"** of which the Upanishads, the Vedanta Sutra (of Sage Baadaraayana) and *Sri Vishnu Sahasranaama* in the Mahabharatha are principal texts.

The subject of *Nirguna Brahman* is thus an extremely abstract, abstruse, formidable, and yet extremely fascinating subject. For centuries it has been the subject of rigorous inquiry found in several scholarly expositions on Vedanta philosophy in traditionally vernacular literature and, otherwise, in heavily academic modern works too. But the discourse being mainly in Sanskrit or Indian vernaculars -- or else in grave, pedantic English commentary written for scholarly or discerning audiences – the mass of ordinary English-speaking laypersons or general laity of Hindus at large in India, who are not so much at ease with Sanskrit, Tamil or Hindi, find it formidable or even incomprehensible. Every human being, high or low, however, does possess an innate spiritual urge to inquire and to know the nature of God or Brahman…. is it **Abstraction** or **Paragon**?

The aim of this book is an attempt to render such a difficult Vedantic topic as intelligible as possible to an average layperson without in any way reducing it to an oversimplification. The method of exposition adopted in this book is in the traditional Upanishadic template of a non-formal but intensely searching **Dialogue** ("*samvaada*") conducted between an imaginary disciple and teacher, one who happens to be an astutely intelligent graduate university-student of Philosophy and other is the "***Unknown Sri Vaishnava***" who plays the role of a friendly academic guide to him.

****

Table of Contents

Dialogue 1: Scholars and Exegetists, Seekers and Mystics. 1

Dialogue 2: The "Tri-Gunas" 9

Dialogue 3: Brahman as "*Nirguna*" in the "Sri Vishnu Sahasranaamam" 16

Dialogue 4: "*Bhagavath-Guna-Darpana*": Mirrored Reflections of Infinite Perfections...................................... 28

Dialogue 5: Conceptions of *Brahman* in Advaita 40

Dialogue 6: A Brief Digression into Post-Sankara Buddhism 56

Dialogue 7: Ramanuja "*darsana*": "*Jagath-Kaaranatvam*" And "*Apprthak-Siddhi*" 70

Dialogue 8: The Polemics of the "*Nirguna*" Debate 81

Epilogue 98

Acknowledgments 102

Bibliography 104

Dialogue 1

Scholars and Exegetists, Seekers and Mystics.

One day a highly intelligent graduate student of Philosophy, who was pursuing a formal academic degree for some years in a local university, posed this question related to Vedanta Philosophy to the *Unknown Sri Vaishnava*:

"*If* Brahman, the Ultimate Reality, has no attributes (*"nirguna brahman"*), how is the Advaitin's statement to be reconciled with the *"anantha kalyaana guna-s,"* the paragon of perfect qualities of the same Brahman the Visishtaadvaitin posits?

The Unknown Sri Vaishnava realized that this student had already reached a certain advanced stage of grasping subtle Vedantic concepts and so decided to proceed to engage the bright young man in a series of dialogues to try and comprehensively account for the concept of Brahman as "nirgunan" and "sagunan" in the two schools of Vedanta: Advaita and Visishtaadvaita.

Below is a transcript of those dialogues conducted over several days.

****

Let this be clear: **Sri Ramanuja** in his magnum opus *"Sri Bhaashya"* (commentary on the **Brahma Sutras**) and his disciple **Sri Vedanta Desika**, in his famous work *"Satadushani"*, are the principal formulators of the position of Visishtaadvaita Vedanta on the question of **Nirguna** and **Saguna Brahman**. They did not seek to *"reconcile"* their position *vis-a-vis* the Advaita Vedantic position on the matter of the Upanishadic Brahman being *"attribute-less"* i.e., bereft of all "*guNa*-s." They instead both spoke of the fulsome "*kalyaana gunas"* (i.e., *auspicious attributes*) of the Upanishad Brahman, the Paragon of limitless perfections.

Ramanuja and Vedanta Desika categorically asserted that Brahman cannot ever conceivably or logically be "nirgunan" in the strictly Advaitic sense --- certainly not in ontological terms nor in terms of characteristics intuited by the human mind. Thus, their philosophical position is not reconciliatory at all; it is categorical and they have based their position firmly on the authority of "sruti" and "smriti" "vaakya-s" as well their well-reasoned interpretation of the "brahma-*sutra*-s".

This topic is an extremely philosophical one. On the part of any student of Vedanta seeking to understand it, he or she will require at least some level of acquaintance with, if not firm grounding in, Vedantic metaphysics, epistemology, formal logic, semantics, and hermeneutics.

I am not a qualified philosopher... not in the formal sense, anyway ... I too am a student of Vedanta like you and so what I will be explaining to you in our conversations should not be regarded as if it were my thesis. It would be foolhardy and dishonest of me to claim here any degree of subject-matter expertise. What I shall be offering to you instead, my dear young man, is only a paraphrase of what I have myself studied and learned from an excellent dissertation on the subject-line by the eminent scholar, (late) **Sri. S.M. Srinivasa Chari** in his book "**Advaita and Visishtadvaita**" (*Motilal Banarasidas Publishers*).

In the fifth chapter in his book, titled *"The Doctrine of Nirguna Brahman"*, Sri S.M.S Chari has comprehensively explained the Advaita Vedanta position on the **Nirguna-Brahman** concept and why Visishtaadvaita Vedanta holds it to be illogical and untenable from the standpoint of the Upanishad and Brahma-Sutra "*vaakya*-s".

The subject is profound, its concepts are difficult to grasp, and the arguments flying about back forth between the Advaita and Vishishtaadvaita proponents are indeed very formidable to comprehend for ordinary intellects unschooled in the traditional intellectual disciplines of "*tarka*", "*meemaamsa*" and "*vyaakarana*".

I shall endeavor therefore to do my best in presenting the subject through paraphrase and summation in as simple and intelligible a manner as possible. But should you, dear young man, at any time midway, find my expositions to be inadequate or unsatisfactory, you should please go straight to the original texts themselves and find answers to your doubts and further questions there. You could begin with S.M.S Chari's book itself and then proceed gradually to journey forth even further and beyond to the ultimate sources of *Sri Bhaashya* of Ramanuja and the *Satadushani* of Vedanta Desika. Along the way, I will also guide you to useful bibliography for your further study.

Besides wanting to simply share with you what I have been able to myself understand about this fascinating question of philosophy, the only other purpose of my being willing to dialogue with you is really to seek a measure of my level of comprehension of it. In that humble spirit of learning, I shall try to answer the various issues you have raised before me to the best of my knowledge, based on what I have learned from my guru and mentors supplemented by whatever of Vedanta literature I have delved into myself.

****

My "*maanaseeka-guru*" (late) *'Vaikunta-vaasi'* **U.Ve. Sri Mukkur Lakshminarasimhachariar (1944-2000 CE)** while expatiating on this topic in some of his widely acclaimed public discourses used to cover it in three cogent and lucid steps:

1. What is meant by "Guna" in the true Vedantic sense?

2. What is meant by "Brahman" in the sense in which the Upanishads have conceived it to be?

3. What is the polemical exchange between the Advaita and Visishtaadvaita schools of Vedanta on the issue of whether Brahman is without "Guna" or abounds in glorious Guna?

In my first dialogue with you, I too propose to structure my presentations on this subject in the same manner as my venerable *maanaseeka-guru* I know used to do.

Now, let us take up **S.No.1. and S.No.2. above**. It would be unnecessary for me to unduly belabor the concept of *Guna* since you, as a student of philosophy, must already be quite familiar with the concept.

Nonetheless, there should be no harm, I believe, in recapitulating the salience of the concept of *Guna* as a matter of prefacing my presentation here. The heart of the entire matter is, of course, only in the **S.No.3. above.** It is what you may call real "*technical stuff*"! It is tough to grasp and a lot of it is taught and learned in universities like yours, in Vedanta academic institutes, punditry circles in religious schools and in Mutts in India and abroad. It is tough because it involves knowing and understanding a great deal of *Tarka (*dialectics*), meemaamsa* (exegesis and hermeneutics) and *vyaakarana (*grammar and semantics*)* and both schools of Vedanta have engaged in them enormously since the times of **Sankara, Sayana, Appayya Dikshita, Ramanuja and Vedanta Desika** --- all of whom are acknowledged giants and stalwarts in their respective schools of Vedanta.

It is not particularly easy for laypeople and laity --- amongst whom both you and I must humbly accept we belong --- to appreciate the lofty, and at times, abstruse issues of metaphysics, dialectics, and formal logic in which the two school and its proponents, engage in and defend their respective "*darsana*-s". Feeble minds cannot sometimes even fully comprehend what these doughty debaters are talking about when they argue (and you might say, sometimes even *hair-split and logic-chop* too!) about *nirguna* and *saguna* Brahman --- the Godhead that is held by one school to be **"attribute-less, formless, nameless, inconceivable Reality"** and, in contrast, by the other school, which holds that Brahman is **"a paragon of the most auspicious attributes"** that can ever be conceived by Man.

While Advaitins and Visishtaadvaitins all do agree, in their respective positions, upon the nature of **Guna** and as well as upon the ***ontological reality* of Brahman** – i.e., Brahman as incontrovertible "**Tattva**" -- what they however wholly disagree upon is whether that very same Brahman is "***guna-ful* or *guna-less*"**!

That disagreement may strike many thinking persons --- I confess it often does so strike me too, and I can say with all due modesty I am not an unthinking person and I know neither are you, my dear young man! --- as nothing more than a disagreement over whether *the glass is half-full or half-empty* ... or as mere semantic disagreement over *Tweedledee and Tweedledum*!

To conclusively decide the question of whether Brahman is *nirgunan* or *sagunan*, it would require one to first know what Brahman is. But then the Upanishads say knowledge of Brahman is entirely experiential and never intellectual. The **Taittiriya Anandavalli** begins in fact by saying: *"He who knows Brahman as Reality, Knowledge and Infinity, knows it to be* **"hidden in the cave of his heart"**.... **("yo vihitam guhaayaam paramey vyomann...")**

So, when Brahman lies hidden *"inside the cave of the human heart"* and can only be known through **direct, personal experience** and **not through impersonal, abstract thought**, then why and how do the two schools of Vedanta consider it fit or even purposeful at all to go on debating *ad infinitum* about a matter that is purely intellectual? What purpose does the attempt to find an answer for the question really serve? Why not just leave it all to the individual soul to experience for itself and realize on its very own the truth about *nirguna* or *saguna* Brahman all by itself?

****

The student smiled and told the Unknown Sri Vaishnava, "Sir, you have accurately read my mind! That is exactly the question that I was about to pose to you too!"

The dialogue thus continued and the Unknown Sri Vaishnava said:

The problem with such questioning is that there can be no conclusive answer for it based on pure cerebration or reasoning.

Metaphysical concepts remain inscrutably metaphysical.... and one cannot arrive at answers for metaphysical questions through any amount of physical exertion of the human intellect or intuition.

"*Sruti*" is thus the sole and final authority in all such spiritual matters and hence the question of whether Brahman is *saguna* or *nirguna* will have to be ultimately decided only on the strength of the scriptural texts (**the Vedas**).'

As S.M.S. **Chari** in his book **"Advaita and Visishtaadvaita"** then explains:

QUOTE

"But here we are faced with a difficulty. There are scriptural texts which speak of Brahman as devoid of qualities (*Svetasvataara, Mundaka, Chandogya, and Brihadaaranyaka Upanishads*, for example), while there are also texts which openly declare Brahman to be qualified by numerous attributes (e.g., the very same sources quoted above with the addition of the *Taittiriya Upanishad* too).

"How are we to overcome such a conflict?

"There are two ways to resolving it.

"One is to accept the validity of both the texts and interpret them in such a way that the apparent conflict does not arise at all. This is the method adopted by the Visishtaadvaitin.

"The other way of solving the difficulty is to ascribe a superior validity to one of the two conflicting texts and deny the other as non-authoritative. The Advaitin who does not agree with the former method adopts this latter (method). Both the texts, he contends, cannot be maintained to be equally valid since they refer to an existent "siddha vastu." Obviously, one of them must be negated as invalid.

"Of the two conflicting texts, saguna and nirguna srutis, which of them are of greater validity?"

UNQUOTE

The Unknown Sri Vaishnava: When we read the above-quoted passage and properly understand what the issue is here between the two contending Vedantic schools, we will not fail to begin realizing slowly that this great debate between Advaita and Visishtaadvaita is not so much about the nature of Brahman being *saguna* or *nirguna*, as much as it is about which set of scriptural texts in the Upanishads is more valid than the other.

Therefore, it is extremely important to first understand, young man, the question you asked me at the very beginning relates to the domain of hermeneutics only; and **it is not really about the *direct, subjective experience of the reality itself called Brahman*.** The debate about this question is really a contest between scholars and professional exegetists... and not really between *seekers*, *saadhakaas* or *upaasakaas*, genuine spiritual mystics…

And if that fact is understood and internalized by all of us, we will never allow ourselves to be swayed, while engaging in the study of this contentious matter, by any strong feelings likely to be aroused in our minds by narrow sectarian persuasion, passion, or conviction in favor of either one argument or the other put forth by these two great Vedantic schools.

Let us always keep in mind during our dialogues that the real search for Brahman by the individual soul (*jeevaatma*) can be conducted only in, and through, a journey on a "***road less traveled.***" It is the road of "*saadhana*" and "*svaanubhava*" (Direct Individual Experience). The other road oft-traveled is a very well-beaten track --- the one that leads only to scriptural knowledge gained through mere scholasticism.

****

Dialogue 2

The "Tri-Gunas"

Let us now turn our attention to the first of the 3-step method of exposition outlined (in Dialogue 1) viz. *knowing the nature of Guna in the true Vedantic sense.*

Many students like you who I know have come up to me on many an occasion and asked challengingly, whether I believed in the principle or reality of the three *'gUNa'— 'sattva,' 'rajas,' and 'tamas''?*

'If yes,' they then went on to demand from me, *'what is the objective basis of your belief?'*

I often responded to such questions half with amusement and half with good-natured mischief.

I usually told them, tongue-in-cheek, *'Yes, I believe in the reality of the 'tri-guNAs.'* The basis of my belief is the **'Bhagavath-Gita**.' There are approximately fifty stanzas in the Gita which are devoted to describing *'sattva,' 'rajas,' and 'tamas'* and how they operate in the world. I have read those stanzas. I find them to be sound and objective conceptually... at least, 'objective' enough on which I can confidently establish my belief in the reality of 'tri-guNA.'

Often my response not only counters but also silences my interrogators. They had awaited and expected me to launch into some long-winded (and thoroughly unconvincing) explanation of how and why I have come to believe in the concept of *'tri-gUna.'* But the moment they hear me say blandly that the **'Gita'** is the fundamental grounding for my belief, the sheer simplicity of my response stops them dead in their tracks. It is not the sort of answer they really anticipated, and it effectively takes the wind out of their sails. They are also silenced by the response since few amongst them have even a nodding acquaintance with the fifty-odd '*shlOkA*-s' of the **Gita** I am talking about. Stymied thus by their own ignorance and realizing the futility of engaging me in further discussion, they usually decide it is far better to leave me alone.

Thus, have I, on many an occasion, managed to maneuver and escape being dragged, quite against my wishes, into verbose discussions on one of the most talked-about but little understood principles of Vedantic philosophy— the *'tattva' of 'tri-gUNa.'*

If my arithmetic is not wrong, there are, give or take a few, about sixty-five '*shlOkA*-s' in all in the **Gita** devoted to examining in detail the subject of '*tri-gUNa*':

In **chapter 7,** Krishna while explaining the nature of the material world ('*prakruti*') brings up the subject for the first time. He does it quite suddenly in **stanzas 12 and 13** too almost springing a surprise on Arjuna (throughout the Gita, we see this as a common occurrence i.e., Krishna taking poor Arjuna, his student, suddenly by surprise by introducing a new idea or new strand of thought in the middle of a long exposition on another theme. You, however, dear young man, should not be anxious for I shall not pull tricks on you similarly as Sri Krishna did with Arjuna!):

tribhir-gUNa-mayyair-bhAvair

abhi sarvamidam jagat

mOhitam nAbhi-jAnAti
mAmEbhyah param-avyayam.

The nature of all the world
and all this universe
Mired as they are in the three 'gUNa-s,'
is caused by them.
They veil the world
from Me—
I am beyond them
Eternal and unchanged!

****

Then in **chapter 14** again, beginning with **stanza 5 through 18**, Krishna introduces Arjuna to the concepts of *Sattva, Rajas, and Tamas*. He provides us their definitions, explains their properties, and even constructs a cause-effect matrix to help open Arjuna's eyes to the reality of the *'tri-gUNa-s.'* Arjuna then beholds and recognizes the world in a new light. Slowly he begins to understand it all in terms of the threefold elements of *'tri-gUNas.'*

Reading all those stanzas carefully and reflecting deeply upon them, we too begin to understand that *Sattva, Rajas, and Tamas* are great powerful Forces indeed acting upon and, in this world, in much the same way perhaps as we know, say, **gravity, magnetic field**s, or **radioactivity,** rule this world.

None can ever grasp or clutch at a handful of gravity but everyone and everything in this world is bound by it (*'badhnAti'*). Similarly, you cannot hold a **magnetic field** within the palm of the hand, but just go near a source of magnetism and see what happens to you; it will envelop you like an octopus embraces its prey. Again, you never actually get to see **X-rays, radio waves, alpha, gamma, or infra-red rays** in the air around you, but nonetheless, they are all out there all the time—in every single breath, you take in and out, every blessed moment of your life.

There is no way that the *'tri-guNA-s'* can be avoided, no more than one can avoid gravity in this world. But, quite like gravity itself, the *'tri-guNA-s'* can be overcome and made to work to our advantage or to even serve our chief and desired purposes in life. If you climb to a height and are careless enough to slip, gravity will surely ensure your painful fall. But if you know and master the art of sky-gliding, you can use the same force of gravity to your advantage and take to the great skies. In the same way, although we have no power whatsoever over *Sattva, Rajas, and Tamas*, we can nonetheless learn to use and exploit them wisely and profitably, to further our own true purposes in life.

****

Next, **in chapter 17 of the Gita**, Krishna adopts a very scientific approach in explaining the operation of the '*tri-gUNa-s'* in the world. Starting with **stanzas 7, 8, 9, and 10** and proceeding step-by-step—beginning with **stanza 20 all the way through stanza 40**—Krishna expounds the way *Sattvas, Rajas, and Tamas* function in this world (and within the body-mind-soul complex of man). Like a cold, clinical, and methodical professor, Krishna gives Arjuna a wonderful lesson, full of elegance, profundity, and penetrative insight into the working of the *'tri-gUNa-s.'*

You cannot study the great forces of the world or understand how they work through mere conceptual or theoretical constructs or cerebral speculation alone. You must instead learn to see them as they operate or function in the real world.

Now how to do that?

Newton studied gravity and motion through serious inquiry into why as simple an object as an apple falls from a tree to the ground. Faraday studied magnetism by carefully studying how iron-filings react when brought within the proximity of a magnetic field. Nuclear scientists study wave radiation by watching how radio-active substances (like say, uranium isotopes) react under process.

The same method and approach may be used to study '*tri-gUNa-s*' too—i.e., we may study it by studying the behavior of objects and entities upon which the forces of '*tri-gUNa*' operate. To study *Rajas* and to understand how it operates, you simply turn your attention to objects/entities/persons upon whom *Rajas* is acting. To study *Tamas*, all you must do is to study the behavior of objects/entities/persons that are recognized to be under the powerful influence of *Tamas*.

To help us readily and easily recognize the many categories of objects/entities in the world upon which the '*tri-gUNa-s*' are acting, Krishna provides in the Gita many useful illustrations and typical case studies. These, in effect, provide us (as well as they did Arjuna at Kurukshetra) great psychological insight into the phenomenon of '*tri-gUNa.*' Krishna in effect tells Arjuna this in as many words:

'You can understand "tri-gUNa-s" by simply taking up the careful study of the behavior of one who is under the grip of Sattva, Rajas, and Tamas. Watch what he worships most in life [*"shraddha"*]. Watch how he goes about "worshipping" in life [*"yajantE"*]. Enquire into the kinds of food he eats and keep a tag on his eating habits [*"aahAra-niyamam"*]. Observe too how he gives away gifts/charity in life [*"dAna"*]. Keenly take note of the extent and quality of sacrifices [*"yagnya," "tapas"*] he makes in life. Watch too how he speaks [*"vAkyam"*] and the quality of his utterances. Focus too on the many ways his mind [*"mana-prasAdah:"*] works and manifests itself in his actions. All these, O Arjuna, are clear and categorical pointers to the operation of the *"tri-gUNas"* . . . Study them and you shall unlock the mystery of the *"tri-gUNa-s"* and by doing so shall you be enabled to conquer them, go beyond them, become fit for Bhakti-yoga experience and ultimately reach my State of Brahman!':

> *mAm cha yO'avya abhichArENa*
> *bhakti-yOgEna sEvatE;*
> *sa gUNAn samateet-tyaitAn*
> *brahma-bhUyAya kalpatE (14.26)*
>
> He who serves Me with Bhakti
> By crossing beyond the GunAs
> Becomes fit and ready
> For the state of Brahman!

****

In the concluding **chapter 18 of the Gita**, in **stanzas 7 through 10** and later in **stanzas 20 through 40,** Krishna explains to Arjuna how the *'tri-gUNa-s'* may be overcome by man and how such conquest paves the way for attaining the state of directly experiencing Brahman.

In a thrilling and final peroration in the Srimadh **Bhagavath-Gita**, Krishna explains how even the most precious possessions of man, his **Buddhi** (intellect), and **Manas** (mind) are subject to the thrall and influence of the '*tri-gUNa-s*' and how even the knowledge (*GnyAna*) that we gain and come to possess in our earthly existence is conditioned and clouded or colored by the three-fold characters of *Sattva, Rajas, and Tamas.*

To go beyond the *'tri-gUNa-s'* is to conquer them. It is possible for man and that is one of the principal themes of the eighteenth chapter of the Gita. It *is* possible to overcome the *'tri-gUNA-s'* just as it is possible to conquer *gravity, magnetism, or radioactivity in this world.*

Man's conquest of *'tri-gUNa-s'* involves **'nyAsa'**—renunciation or surrender ('**parithyadja**'). This too, says Krishna, is of three types: *Sattvic, Rajasic, and Tamasic* and then urges us to make sure, as much as possible, to adhere in life to the '*Sattvic mode of Renunciation.*' And that mode lies in performing your duties in a spirit of complete and absolute '**nyAsa**'—acting without expectation of returns, fruit, or reward, or else surrendering them all to the Almighty, *'sarvam sri KrishnArpaNam.'*

Thus, briefly sketched, ends **Gita's** magnificent treatment of the subject of *'tri-gUNa-s.'*

A deep understanding of the concept and reality of *'tri-gUNa-s'* is very essential to the practice of the Vedantic faith and in trying to understand the concept of both "*nirguna*' and '*saguna*' Brahman. Those few who succeed in that understanding, attain the state of experiencing Brahman, says Krishna in the Gita and it is, in fact, what the Upanishads too echo. There will be many who fail and will fall short of realizing Brahman; but still, they will be able to achieve something valuable out of all their effort— viz.: a fuller understanding of the larger world around them and of their true inner selves.

****

Dialogue 3

Brahman as *"Nirguna"* in the "Sri Vishnu Sahasranaamam"

The student next asked the *Unknown Sri Vaishnava*:

"Having summarized the Vedantic conception of the *"tri-gunas,"* can you now please proceed to similarly expatiate upon how the Advaita and Visishtaadvaita schools have conceived the Upanishadic Brahman (as outlined in S.No.2 in your preamble (in Dialogue 1)?"

Thus, began the third Dialogue with the student.

****

The **Bhagavath-Gita** is a *"smriti"* text from the great *"itihaasa"*, the **Mahabharatha** which is regarded by all authorities of all schools of Vedanta as verily the *"fifth Veda"* since the spiritual verities and ethical precepts it contains are derivates, amplifications, and elaborations of its source, the Vedas themselves. Therefore, in the **Gita,** if the reality of the *tri-guna* is categorically stated by **Sri Krishna** to be true, it cannot be controverted or quibbled about. The existence of "*prakruti*" ((the material and phenomenal world -- i.e., the universe of all **"acit"** (insentient) and **"cit"** (sentient) entities)) -- as an ontological reality is a fact (*sath*); and that it is characterized by all manner of *imperfections, infirmities, frailties, and impermanence* engendered by the *"tri-Gunas"* --- *'sattva', "rajas"* and *"tamas"* --- is also a fact.

In the very same Mahabharatha, *the 5th Veda,* there is another text well known to many as the celebrated **"Sri Vishnu Sahasranaamam".** This text is a litany of "**1000** sacred names" (*naama*) of **Bhagavaan Vishnu**, the one whom the Upanishads hail as the Brahman. These one thousand "*naama-s*" are held to be very sacred in the Hindu faith because each of them represents one specific "*guna*" of the Brahman; and the *one thousand names,* each singly and collectively, denote the various unique and excellent "*guna-s*" or qualities/attributes of the Upanishadic Brahman.

While in the Bhagavath Gita it is Divinity itself, in the avatar of Sri Krishna, that expatiates upon the *"guna-visesha"* of the entire universe of "*prakruti*", in the Sri Vishnu Sahasranaama we find a mortal, in the person of the venerable grandsire (*Pitaamahaar*), **Sri Bheeshmaachaarya,** who through *1000 names* in a long, sacred litany of **107 shlokas** in Sanskrit, revealed to humankind the manifold "*guna*-s" of the Supreme Divine Being known to the Vedas as *Brahman* or Vishnu.

In the Visishtaadvaita Vedantic School, the **Sri Vishnu Sahasranaama** holds a pre-eminent position as not only a religious text of sacred chants but also a deeply philosophical one. It is given the status of an outstanding scriptural authority since it emphatically affirms the fundamental axiom of Visishtaadvaita metaphysics: Brahman is a Being full of innumerable attributes (*guna*) of excellence and perfections (*anantha-kalyaana-guna-ganaan*).

Since an infinitude of perfections is almost impossible to be conceived or fully comprehended in the absolute sense by even the best of human intellects *(buddhi sankocham)*, the only way to grasp and realize the essential "*guna-s"*/attributes of Brahman is to contemplate upon a finite number such as, say, one thousand **"mirrored reflections"** of them. Which is exactly what the *Sahasranaama* does. Just as an array of mirrors reflects an infinite number of images of objects placed before it, the *Sahasranaama* too *"mirror reflects",* so to say, the *infinitude of "kalyaana-guna-s"* of Brahman. This is why the *Vishnu*

Sahasranaama is called **"bhagavath guna darpana"**, the word *"darpana"* in Sanskrit meaning 'mirror'.

The *Vishnu Sahasranaama* thus captures a thousand attributes of Vishnu in a thousand names, strings them all together in phonemes and syllables known as the *"1000 naama-s"* and invests each of them with sacred meaning, with spiritual significance as mantra, as as well as with the Truth attested by the Upanishads about there being only one supreme Godhead, the *Brahman*.

One of the most celebrated theologists of the Visishtaadvaita school of Vedanta, the 12th-century CE disciple of Ramanujacharya, **Sri Paraashara Bhattar,** thus took up the *Vishnu Sahasranaamam* and wrote an enlightening commentary on it aptly titled **"Bhagavath-Guna-Darpanam",** explaining the beauty and profundity of the 1000 "*guna*-s" of Vishnu as Brahman, each represented by a unique and sweet-sounding sacred "*naama*".

****

It is ironic that the Sri Vishnu Sahasranaamam, being a litany of 1000 *naama-s mirror-reflecting* the infinitude of perfections of Brahman, does not however use the common Sanskrit proper noun "*Sagunan*" as one of the "*naama*-s" of Brahman. The name, "*sagunan*," had it been included as one amongst the *"one thousand,"* would have indeed been the most appropriate of all epithets to describe Vishnu. However, it is only the antonym, "*nirgunanan*," that is found in the *Sahasranaamam* litany.

The reason Sri Bheeshmaachaarya did not use the explicit expression "*saguna*" in all probability, was this:

He considered it to be too plain and obvious that Brahman was indeed "*sagunan*".... It was already a *given* and the whole of the Sri Vishnu *Sahasranaama* is indeed about that very fact only. According to Bheeshmaachaarya, it is self-evident truth that Brahman is "*sagunan*". It would have been superfluous and tautological to go on to further say then that it was "*sagunan*". (A *tautology* means using two words, nouns, or phrases to express the same meaning in an unnecessary way).

The litany of a thousand "*naama*-s," however, specifically does include the name of "**nirguna**" to describe Brahman! It appears in the **90th shloka** of the *Vishnu Sahasranaama* that reads as follows:

"*Anur Brihat Krishas Sthulo Gunabhrin Nirguno Mahaan I*

Adhritah Svadhritas Svaasyah Praagvamsho Vamshavardhanah II"

In the above *shloka*, there are a total of **twelve** discrete "*naama*-s" of Brahman that is invoked, and the word "**nirguna**" is the **sixth** --- and it is **the 844th** among the "*one thousand*".

****

If Sri Paraashara Bhattar's **"bhagavath-guna-darpana"** is a pre-eminent theological interpretation of the *Sri Vishnu Sahasranaamam* from the standpoint of Visishtaadavaita

Vedanta, the great **Sri Adi Sankara's** commentary on the same text stands equally tall. It is known the world over to all Advaitins as the celebrated "**Sankara Sahasranaama Bhaashya**".

Any student of Vedanta who finds himself/herself grappling with the question of whether Brahman is "*nirguna* or *saguna*" will find that the most convenient place from which to start a philosophical inquiry into the subject is a comparative study of how the word "**nirguna**" gets interpreted in both the "*bhagavath-guna-darpana*" and the "*sankara-sahasranaama-bhaashya*".

Bhattar's explanation for "*nirguna*" is simple and direct and when paraphrased in English, it reads as below:

"**Brahman (*Vishnu*) does not possess the physical qualities, *Sattva, Rajas, and Tamas*... hence He is "*nirguna*". Though He is in eternal contact with the entire universe (*prakruti*), He is not tainted by its qualities (*tri-guna*).... Such is the indication of this "*naama*".** (vide. *"Sri Vishnu Sahasranaama Stotram")* (B.S. Narasimhachaaryulu -- Minerva Press, New Delhi (2001)

When we turn to Sri Sankara's interpretation of the term "**nirguna**" in his "*bhaashya*", this is what we read (in English translation)

"**He is without the "*guna-s*" of *Prakruti*. The Svetasvataara Upanishad (6.11) says, "*kevalo nirgunas cha....*" i.e., one who is not in contact with "*prakruti*" and is without its "*guna-s*" (*sattva, rajas, and tamas*").....** But then Sankara also adds this interjectory line: ... "**As the "*guna*-s" are unreal, metaphysically, Brahman (*Vishnu*) is "*nirguna*".** --- (vide. **Swami Tapasyaananda** - "*Sri Vishnu Sahasranaamam"* -- Translation into English of Sri Sankaracharya's commentary -- published by Ramakrishna Math, Chennai (1986))

The word "*nirguna*" thus gets interpreted by the Advaitin and Visishtaadvaitin in a vastly different manner according to their respective philosophical conception of Brahman.

****

Student: I am a little confused.

Unknown Sri Vaishnava: Why?

Student: The "*tri-guna-s*" -- "*sattva, rajas and tamas*" -- described by Sri Krishna in the Bhagavath-Gita are *real*. Are they not?

Unknown Sri Vaishnava: Yes.

Student: But it is they that make the nature of "*prakruti*" or the universe inherently imperfect, defective, infirm, and impermanent?

Unknown Sri Vaishnava: Yes.

Student: The Visishtaadvaitin holds the "tri-*guna*-s" are attributes of "*prakruti*" only; and they can never denote "*bhagavath-guna*" --- the paragon of perfections, Brahman?

Unknown Sri Vaishnava: True. You are right. The "*guna*" of Brahman is utterly unlike the "*guna*" of "*prakruti*." And it is, in fact, in that very sense that Brahman is "*nirgunan*" as far as the Visishtaadvaitin is concerned. The word "*nirguna*" is, for the Visishtaadvaitin, a negative description of Brahman i.e., Brahman is "*samasta-heya-pratyaneeka*" --- "**defect-less**." Ramanuja takes the view that **defect-less-ness** or "*heya-pratyaneekatvam*" itself constitutes an essential attribute of Brahman, distinguishing it thus, in fact, from the universe comprising souls and non-sentient matter of *prakruti* which are all characterized by the "*tri-guna-s*."

Student: But that is quite similar to the Advaitin's position too, isn't it? What is the difference?

Unknown Sri Vaishnava: No, not really! The Advaitin agrees with the Visishtaadvaitin that the *tri-guna*-s are not attributes of Brahman and who is thence "*nirgunan*". But then the Advaitin does so for a reason altogether different from that of the Visishtaadvaitin. The Advaitin's reasoning (as can be seen from the Sankara *Sahasranaama bhaashya* above) is in the form of a syllogism. He holds that

Brahman alone is real and that **"*tri-guna-s*"** and "*prakruti*" are both **unreal;** what is unreal can never be an attribute of the real; hence, Brahman is "*nirgunan*".

Student: Then which of the two interpretations of "*nirguna*" is valid?

Unknown Sri Vaishnava: That is a matter for further inquiry.

****

Student: I have then another question.

Unknown Sri Vaishnava: Go ahead, ask.

Student: The Visishtaadvaitin's position (as in Bhattar's interpretation above) is that "*although Brahman is not tainted by the* tri-guna-*s afflicting* prakruti, *he nonetheless remains in eternal contact with the entire universe (*prakruti*) or always integrally related to it....*"

Unknown Sri Vaishnava: Correct.

Student: The Advaitin however, on the contrary, avers that since all "*prakruti*" is unreal and Brahman alone is real, the question of any contact or relation between the two entities does not arise at all. And even much less, therefore, does the question of any taint arising therefrom.

Unknown Sri Vaishnava: Correct.

Student: That is confusing. Which of the two interpretations then is valid?

Unknown Sri Vaishnava: That too is a matter for further inquiry….

****

Student: I have yet another question that baffles me.

Unknown Sri Vaishnava: Go ahead, ask.

Student: Vedantic conceptions of the "*triguna-s*" of "*prakruti*" --*sattva, rajas, and tamas* – are clear to me. You have explained them quite well (in Dialogue 2). But the Visishtaadvaitin also says that the nature of "*bhagavath-guna*" --- in other words, the many-splendored, perfect, and infinite attributes of Brahman which the *Vishnu Sahasranaama* is said to "*mirror reflect*" through a thousand select names -- is entirely different from that of "*prakruti*."

Unknown Sri Vaishnava: That is true. The attributes of Brahman are entirely different from that of "*sattva, rajas, tamas*" that define the nature of the universe, "*prakruti*."

Student: In what way are the two different?

Unknown Sri Vaishnava: That again is a matter for further inquiry.

Student: And I have a corollary to the same question.

Unknown Sri Vaishnava: What is it?

Student: What is the Vedantic meaning of *real* and *unreal*? I raise this question because in the Advaitin's logic, *gunas* being unreal seem to be a very critical factor. I am particularly keen to know if "*unreal*" means "*non-existent*"?

Unknown Sri Vaishnava: It's a good question you have asked on the semantics of Vedantic discourse and the problems it sometimes poses while dealing with the English translation of Sanskrit terms. Let us dispose of it right here and now rather than postponing it to later inquiry.

The Vedantic term for "non-existent" is "*a-sath*" and the term for "unreal" is "*mithya*" or, more popularly, "*maaya*", though the two terms are not strictly interchangeable.

From our common experience of the world, it is possible to easily distinguish between the following:

- An entity can *exist* and yet appear to be *unreal*. E.g., A man suffers from jaundice, sees everything around him in a haze of yellow; all that he sees does *exist*, but their perceived yellowness is *unreal*, is it not?

- An entity can appear to be very **real** and yet **not exist** at all. E.g. the classic rope and snake analogy of the Advaitin. The rope is very *real* but in its appearance like a snake, the snake does not exist at all.

- An entity can appear to **both exist and be real** ... and yet may **not be true**. E.g. my "*manaseeka achaarya*", **Sri Mukkur Lakshminarasimhachariar** used to cite this amusing example. A very pious, orthodox Sri Vaishnava – in traditional garb, shaven-headed except for a knotted tuft and with all the 12-great holy marks smeared upon his body-- traveled in a taxi to a certain destination. On reaching there, he moved to pay the metered-fare with a 100-rupee note. The taxi driver demurred saying he did not have change and demanded that he be paid the fare with the exact tender. The pious Sri Vaishnava wanting to change the 100-rupee note had then no choice really but to stride into a nearby restaurant to request the cashier there to favor him with smaller denominations for the 100-rupee note. He collected the change and returned with it to pay the taxi-driver off. Now, a bystander who had just then passed by, saw the pious Sri Vaishnava as he was exiting the restaurant. Shocked by what he witnessed, he shook his head to himself in disbelief and disgust and thought to himself: *"Oh God! What is this world coming to! An orthodox, pious Sri Vaishnava Brahmin like him too these days visits roadside restaurants… and that too a non-vegetarian one serving meat! God save this world! How morals have fallen!"*

Here in this incident, the pious appearance of the Sri Vaishnava is *an existent reality*. That he entered the non-vegetarian restaurant and exited it too is *real*… But then the bystander who witnessed it all and concluded that the pious man, therefore, must have consumed meat in the restaurant ... is that *true*?

Vedantic epistemology recognizes all the above three situations of human experience and the challenges that each poses to our ability to establish whether an entity or event is ***true, existent, and real*** ... or ***whether it is untrue, non-existent, and unreal***. To each of the three cases, it applies three modes of inquiry.

The first is "*pratyaksham*" or **Perception**. The second is "*anumaanam*" or **Inference.** And then lastly there is "*sruti*" or **Vedic Revelation**. Beyond these 3 means ("*pramaana*") that aid us in settling the question of ***truth, reality, and existence***, there is no other humanly possible way.

So, turning to your question i.e. if it can be held that "*gunas*" being *unreal,* could also mean they are *non-existent,* the answer is that *it is not necessarily always so*. It is always a matter of determination ... i.e. since Perception and/or Inference both can be fallible. The ***Vedic "sruti"*** however, is held to be infallible and hence it is the final recourse and arbiter to settle matters of *reality, existence, and truth* when both Perception (*pratyaksham*) and Inference (*anumaanam*) fail.

Is your doubt cleared?

Student: Yes, sir, thank you. Let us please proceed. But I have asked you three questions each of which you have said is to be answered only through "*further inquiry*". How begins such a line of inquiry?

Unknown Sri Vaishnava: For the first two questions you asked, one must go and search the "*sruti pramaana*" – the authoritative texts of the Upanishads and Brahma Sutras. Relying on the aid provided by the Acharyas of both schools of Vedanta, we can grasp the matter by understanding how they have interpreted the texts.

For the third and last of your questions, the answer can be found in the *Vishnu Sahasranaama* itself. So let us discuss it first.

****

Dialogue 4

"Bhagavath-Guna-Darpana": Mirrored Reflections of Infinite Perfections

The Unknown Sri Vaishnava began dialoguing with the student with the following opening remarks:

"It is indisputable that *"sruti vaakya-s"* – the word of the revealed scripture, Veda and Upanishad – alone are the *"pramaana,"* or the authoritative basis on which the *Vishnu Sahasranaama* text was inspired. It is however accepted by both the Advaitin and the Visishtaadvaitin that the Sahasranaama being a *"smriti"* text i.e., an auxiliary to the *'sruti,'* is for that very reason alone, of less relative weight as *"pramaanaa"* than *'sruti'*.

Now, as far as your second and third questions are concerned, Advaitin's argument would be that the *"nirgunatvam"* of Brahman cannot be properly decided, one way or the other, on the basis of a *"smriti"* text such as the *Sahasranaama*. It is only a valid interpretation of the *"sruti"* texts themselves that can establish the matter. Interpretation of *sruti* texts thus becomes a deeply philosophical issue between the two schools. Let us not discuss it now but later after we have first examined the third question you raised *viz.*:

The attributes of Brahman are entirely different from that of the "tri-gunas" (i.e. "sattva, rajas, and tamas") that define the nature of the universe known as "prakruti." In what way are the two different?

****

The answer is found articulated in Visishtaadvaita Vedanta and within the context of the Vishnu Sahasranaama itself. We have thus saved us the trouble of going to great distances to refer to particular "*sruti*" texts and to belabor their interpretations by two vastly different Vedantic schools.

The Visishtaadvaitin begins plainly by asking the Advaitin a pointed question regarding the matter:

"You accept the Vishnu Sahasranaama to be valid "*smriti*" "*pramaana*;" and you even quote it to elucidate your own view of Brahman being "*nirguna*." Yet, at the same time, you aver that the interpretation of the "one thousand *naama*-s" in the "*bhagavath-guna-darpana*" cannot be accepted as reflecting the real "*guna*-s" of Brahman – "*metaphysically speaking*," that is -- since the "*gunaa*-s" themselves are unreal!"

"If what you say is true, then the Vishnu Sahasranaama must itself be wholly unreal since it is, after all, nothing but only "*mirrored reflections*" of what is unreal "*bhagavath-guna*"?

"So then, how can that, which to you is unreal, be able to reveal what is true… i.e. the truth and reality of Brahman?!

"If the "*smriti*" as a "*pramaana*" itself is not real, how can even discussion on Vedantic metaphysics be continued meaningfully between you and me?" (*Ref: "Vaada #9*" of Vedanta Desika's "*satadushani*"). Unless the "*pramaana*" itself is real, no metaphysical investigation can be conducted and, consequently, no truth too can be established."

****

The fundamental issue in the matter between the Advaitin and the Visishtaadvaitin is therefore only this:

Whether the Vishnu Sahasranaama qualifies to be what Vedantic scholars call as an "***upabrhmana***": a valid elucidation of the meaning of the *sruti* scriptural texts.

If it is not "*upabrhmana*" then the Advaitin should have nothing to do with it. He should be rejecting it outright since it deals with "*unreal*" attributes of Brahman.

But then the Advaitin *does not* reject the Sahasranaama. He quotes the text, in fact, to support his metaphysics of total negation of attributes i.e., "*nirgunatvam*"/ "*nirvisesham*," does he not? By doing so, does he not put himself in the same position as one who wants to *eat the cake and have it too*? How can the Sahasranaamam that has been said to be dealing with *unreal* things, in the same breath, also be said to be valid "*upbrhmana*" to establish Reality? Is it not absurd to suggest that the *real and true* can be established through what is said to be *unreal and untrue*?!

The Advaitin's reply to the question is often framed like this:

Although a "*pramaana*" can be unreal in character, and even be found to be dealing with illusory "*guna*-s," it can still reveal what is real.

In our ordinary experience, the Advaitin will continue, a rope is mistaken to be a snake and that causes fear. The rope is *real*... but the snake and the fear are *unreal and untrue*. But when what is *unreal* is shown to be ... or is realized to be ... *unreal*, then reality alone remains; nothing else but the *real* exists thereafter. Therefore, from the *unreal*, it is possible to show what is *real* and realize it too. The Vishnu Sahasranaamam serves our Advaitin's purpose only in such a capacity.

The epistemological questions arising from the above-contested issue between the Advaitin and the Visishtaadvaitin are very thorny and vexatious. And it is from this point onwards that they both launch into an exhaustive and combative debate involving "*vyaakarana*" and "*tarka*". They then delve into the relative merits of the three distinct kinds of "*pramaana*" in Vedanta philosophy viz. Perception (*pratyaksham*), Inference (*anumaana*), and

Revelatory Scripture (*aagama*) to apprehend the nature of Reality.

The "*satadushani*" of Vedanta Desika is a compilation of all those debates and inquiries set in the form of "*100 vaada-s*" ("*sata*", means "100" and "*vaada dushani*" means "disputations"). Out of the one hundred disputations, as the title of the "*grantha*" (work) suggests, actually only 66 "*vaada*-s" are found recorded in it. The remaining thirty-four are lost.

The debates between the two schools are indeed profound, formidable, and rapier-sharp. It is not my intention here in our dialogues to either try and paraphrase or summarize the thrust and parrying, the punch and counterpunching, or the various philosophical theses and anti-theses put forth and back by proponents and adversaries in that debate. Our conversation must stay firmly focused on the subject of "*nirguna Vs saguna*" conception alone. A study of the dialectical polemics between the two Vedantic schools must be deferred to some other occasion in the future.

(If, however, young man, you are curious or keen to know the details of those debates, you are referred to "*Vaada 9* through *Vaada 30*" of Vedanta Desikan's "*satadushani*". (See also Chapters 1 through 4 of S.M.S. Chari's book, "***Advaita and Visishtadvaita***").

****

Unknown Sri Vaishnava: It is sufficient for me to say here that Vedanta Desikan establishes the Visishtaadvaitin view most convincingly. He shows how and why the Advaitin is being illogical in claiming a "*smriti pramaana*" (like the Sri Vishnu Sahasranaama, in the instant case), to be valid "*upabrhmana*" when he, at the same time, insists that Brahman, about which the text speaks, is "*nirguna*" (attribute-less) and "*nirvisesha*" (undifferentiated). The Vishnu Sahasranaama, which is explicit in speaking about the "*savisesha*" or "*visesha vibhuti*" aspects or attributes of

Brahman, is therefore not in consonance with the Advaitin's theory of Reality at all.

Vedanta Desikan's very cogent reasons and arguments adduced for that position are given below:

For the sake of argument, if we grant the "*sruti*" indeed does seek to establish the Brahman to be devoid of all determinations (attributes), then whatever is sought to be revealed or elucidated by a *smriti* text such as the Sahasranaamam becomes futile, meaningless, and absurd .... Bheeshmaachaarya, who revealed the "*1000 naama-s*", while lying bleeding to death on a bed of arrows after being slain on the battlefield of Kurukshetra, was only wasting his time....! Why? Because the very express purpose of this "*smriti*" text is to reveal what the *determinations (visesha)* of the Brahman are. That is precisely the stated purpose of the Sahasranaamam; its intent is to "*reflect*" the many *guna-visesha-s* inherent in Brahman.

If, however it is argued that a *smriti* like the Sahasranaamam establishes what the Advaitin claims is the sole truth viz. "*nirvisesha*" Brahman as revealed by "*sruti*, then, in that case, no *smriti* including the Sahasranaamam can ever qualify to be '*upabrhmana*'.

As S.M.S Chari explains in his book, "*the smriti-s and puraanaa-s are regarded as "upabrhmana-s" in as much as they subserve the scripture in the form of either pointing out the specific nature of what has been obtained in the sruti or making clear what is vague.*" If the Vishnu Sahasranaama, however, were to be held as teaching anything else independently as proof of "nirguna Brahman," it cannot hold the status it does -- as "*upabrhmana.*"

When the Advaitin goes further to assert that a *smriti*, such as the Vishnu Sahasranaama, is merely a **restatement** of the "*sruti vaakya*-s" that he quotes or interprets, the "*satadushani*" counters him by pointing out that *restatement of what has already been said conclusively serves no* *purpose*. And it so happens that, etymologically speaking, the Sanskrit term *"upabrhmana"* is not synonymous with *restatement* at all.

Artist impression of the Satadushani debates between Vedanta Desika and adversaries

Arguing thus as he did above, Vedanta Desika clarified that it is not logically possible to uphold *smriti*-s, itihaasa and *puraana* (the Sahasranaamam, in our example), as '*upabrhmana*' **unless** it is first admitted that Brahman spoken about in the scriptural "*sruti*-s" is endowed with infinite attributes and "*vibhuti*-s" (i.e., "*visesha*-s" or manifold determinations). The attributes and *vibhutis* of Brahman, which cannot be ordinarily known and realized through the "*sruti vaakya*" *are* revealed to us by *smriti-texts* and hence, they are aptly called '*upabrhmanas*' in the true sense of the term. They are elucidations -- or, as Sri Paraashara Bhattar termed them, they are "**reflecting mirrors**" or "*bhagavath-guna-darpana*" of what has already been said in the '*sruti.*'

****

The Unknown Sri Vaishnava next told the student:

Listen carefully now. If you keep in mind the arguments ("*vaada*") of the *Satadushani* alluded to above, you will easily understand the answer provided by the Visishtaadvaitin to the specific question you raised:

"How are the "*triguna-s*" of "*prakruti*" –'*sattva, rajas* and *tamas*' -- different from the "*mirrored reflection*" ("*darpana*") of "*bhagavath-guna*", the divine qualities?'

The "*triguna*-s" of *sattva*, *rajas,* and *tamas* that characterize "*prakruti*" are not unreal as the Advaitin claims. While the entire universe or "*prakruti*" is beset by "*triguna*-s," Brahman remains however untouched and untainted by it. And it is only for that reason alone that Brahman has been described in the Sahasranaaman as "*nirgunan*." Such is the Visishtaadvaitic standpoint.

The question arises: *What is the "Visishtaadvaitic standpoint"?* It is this: When we say Brahman is full of "*guna-vibhuthi"* and we also say that this "*prakruti*" too is full of "*triguna-s*," we should not be misunderstood to be implying that the attributes of *sattva*, *rajas* and *tamas* found in the universe are also to be found in Brahman…. or that the attributes of Brahman are in any sort of way akin to those of "*prakruti*."

****

The *44th Peetaadhipathi (pontiff) of Sri Ahobila Math* **Srimad Mukkur Azhagiyasingar** (1897-1992 CE) in one of his many brilliant epistles (*"arul mozhi"*) lucidly explained the fundamental difference between the two metaphysical concepts of *"triguna"* and *"bhagavath-guna"*. It is worth quoting him *in extenso* here as follows:

QUOTE

"First, let me explain what is meant by *"prakruthi."* That ontological entity that is the cause of all elements of nature created and from which they emanated too viz. *Space, Fire, Wind, Water, and Earth* is called *"prakruthi."*

"Milk, curd, butter, ghee, etc. are all mere derivatives of a single substance, aren't they? Do you know that substance? Let me tell you. It is nothing but grass or hay upon which cows feed and they are verily the origin of all dairy products like milk etc. Likewise, that from which the natural elements,

Spatial Ether, Fire, Water, Earth, and *Wind* all emanate is called *Prakruthi*.

"Let me tell you a bit more about *Prakruthi* …. Listen with rapt attention, please.

"Everything that exists in the universe, right from the high heavenly realms of "*brahmaloka*" down to our lowest terrestrial domains, without any exceptions, all become extinct at a certain point in time. During that time of cosmic dissolution, there exist an infinite number of souls which are yet to attain "*moksha*." The souls attach themselves to a (certain) primordial ontological substance just as one might imagine tiny particles of gold-dust fastening themselves to a great big ball of molten wax. That primordial substance, *moola-prakruthi* that is thus admixed with such an assortment of all unredeemed soulful entities is known as "***Tamas***." *Tamas*, while remaining bereft of association with unredeemed souls (*baddha jeevaatmaa*-s), is known as "*prakruthi*."

"From one part of "*prakruthi*" is caused an entity called *Mahat*. From *Mahat* gets created an entity called "*Ahankaaram*" or the Ego (i.e., the primordial sense of "**I-ness**"). "It is from the Ego that is then caused the physical and facultative human sense organs (eyes/ sight, ears/hearing, nose/smell, etc. and the mind) which are eleven in number.

"From another part of "*prakruthi*" emerges – in the way as we all know fresh curd emerges from milk in fermentation -- an entity which in its nascent state is called "*aakaasa*" or Spatial Ether. From the *nascent state of Ether* emerges another state that is *evolved Ether*. From the evolved ethereal state then emerges *nascent natural element*, Wind (*vaayu*), and from which, in turn, emerges the *evolved element* of Wind… And therefrom, again similarly emerges *nascent and evolved* Fire (*agni*), *nascent* Water and *evolved* Water (*jala*), *nascent* Earth and *evolved* Earth (*prithvi*).

"It is through such cosmic process of successive *creation and evolution* of the natural elements that *Bhagavaan* causes the *twenty-four different "tattva-s" or "realities"* to emerge and constitute the substrate of all existence in the universe.

"It is from the substratum of the primordial 24 "*tattvas*' that every "*jeevaatmaa*" (*baddha*) comes into being once again in Creation. In both form and character, the soul acquires the earthly incarnation it deserves by dint of its own unredeemed past deeds viz. its own legacy of an accumulated, unexhausted karmic stock of both "*paapa*" and "*punnya*": evil and virtuous deeds. *Bhagavaan* himself thus inheres into all bodily forms and remains universally immanent within all souls, as their sole protector.

"Next, let me explain the metaphysical entity called "*suddha sattvam*" which you must all try to understand by exerting your intellects a bit.

"The entity called "*prakruti*" that has been explained above comprises three fundamental spiritual essences or qualities called "*guNa*." There are three such primordial "*gunas*": **Sattva, Rajas,** and **Tamas**. The ontological entity called "*suddha-sattva*" is that which is completely devoid of both "*rajas*" and "*tamas*" and is replete with the "*sattva guna*" alone. That is precisely why this entity has come to be termed "*suddha sattva*" – the spiritual-essence that is pristine in the absolute sense. (The *triguna*-s of *prakruti* wax and wane alternatively from time to time (*kaala*), from one circumstance to another, and from one existential condition to another (*stithi*). But "*suddha sattvam*" is never subject to such vagaries of "*kaala*" or vicissitudes of "*stithi*." It remains eternally as pure spiritual essence).

"Every being or thing that exists in *Sri Vaikuntam* (the abode of *Bhagavaan*) is made up of this very same absolutely pristine spiritual-substance called "*suddha-sattva*." In other words, all heavenly beings such as *nithya-suri-s, jeevaatmaa-s* that have attained liberation (*mukthi*),

Bhagavaan himself, as well as all heavenly establishments such as the towers, ramparts, mansions, hallways, and all manner of heavenly structures there –all those are constituted wholly and solely by this supra-ethereal "*suddha-sattvam*."

"No part of what the primordial substance is called "*moola-prakruthi*" is to be found in the realm of Brahman called *Sri Vaikuntam* which is pervaded wholly and solely by "*suddha-sattva*" alone. Conversely, the supra-ethereal substance called "*suddha-sattva*," which is verily the warp-and-woof of the heavenly realm of *Sri Vaikuntam*, is never to be found in the terrestrial worlds.

"Outside those universal realms pervaded entirely by "*suddha-sattva"* do lie the realms where it is "*prakruthi*" that is all-pervasive. And *vice versa*, wherever in the cosmic spaces "*prakruthi*" does not pervade, there it is "*suddha-sattva*" that is all-pervasive.

UNQUOTE

A careful study of the above ideas and explications should now give you, my dear young man, a clear understanding of the sense in which the epithet or *divya-naama* of "*nirguna*" in the Sri Vishnu Sahasranaamam gets ascribed by the Visishtaadvaitin to Brahman and its nature; and how it differs so fundamentally from how Advaitin interprets it.

(a) Without in any way suggesting or asserting that "*sattva, rajas* or *tamas*" are unreal; *(b)* without in any way suggesting that the "1000 *naama*-s" in the litany are even remotely redolent of '*triguna*'; *(c)* without in any way giving rise to as much as even a niggling suspicion that Brahman in being called "*nirguna*" might well be … as the Advaitin believes … a null-entity devoid of any "*guna*"; *(d)* without in any way giving rise to doubts in our minds that the attributes ("*anantha-kalyaana-guna*") of Brahman perhaps bear some comparison to, and are not unlike the "*triguna-s*" that characterize "*prakruti*"…. without any such ambiguities, the *Sri Vishnu Sahasranaamam* extols the "*suddha-sattva guna-*

s" of the Upanishadic Brahman alone. It enumerates them by "*mirroring*" "*one thousand*" examples of "*suddha-sattva-guna-s*" in "*one thousand*" "*naama-s*" in mantra form. It is for that very reason that the Sahasranaamam is held to be very sacred litany by one all.

As recorded in the great Mahabharata, Sri. Bheeshmaachaarya, the great devotee of Sri Krishna, in his dying moments on the battlefield of Kurukshetra, directly experienced the reality of Brahman. Drawing from that experience, he gave his sworn testimony on **"suddha-sattvam"** as being the ontologically essential attribute of the Ultimate Reality, the Supreme Brahman.

Earlier (in Dialogue 2), we came across this *shloka* in Bhagavath Gita:

> *mAm cha yO'avya abhichArENa*
> *bhakti-yOgEna sEvatE;*
> *sa gUNAn samateet-tyaitAn*
>
> *brahma-bhUyAya kalpatE (14.26)*

> He who serves Me with Bhakti
> By crossing beyond the GunAs
> Becomes fit and ready
> For the state of Brahman!

From Bheeshmaacharya's experience and example, you should now be able to surely understand what is spoken of by Sri Krishna as the "*crossing beyond the Guna-s.*" It means only this: transcending the "*tri-gunas*" of "*prakruti*" and entering the eternal state of "*suddha-sattva*" in Sri Vaikuntam.

Student: It appears to me from what you have explained above that the term "*nirgunan*" should perhaps be taken to mean "***beyond gunas***" rather than '**without gunas**'. Would this understanding be correct?

Unknown Sri Vaishnava: That is certainly the view of the Visishtaadvaitin.

****

Dialogue 5

Conceptions of *Brahman* in Advaita

The student reminded the Unknown Sri Vaishnava that *"further inquiry"* into the following two questions was promised and still remained to be addressed:

1. The word "*nirguna*" is for the Visishtaadvaitin, a negative description of Brahman i.e., Brahman being "*samasta-heya-pratyaneeka*". Ramanuja takes the view that **defectlessness** or "*heya-pratyaneekatvam*" itself constitutes an essential attribute of Brahman, distinguishing it thus, in fact, from the universe comprising the souls and non-sentient matter of *prakruti*.

The Advaitin agrees with the Visishtaadvaitin but not for the same reason. For the latter, because the tri-guna's *are* ***not*** *attributes of Brahman*, Brahman qualifies as "*nirgunan*". The Advaitin's reasoning is altogether different: As seen in the Sankara *Sahasranaama bhaashya*, the Advaitin holds that the "*guna-s*" are themselves ***unreal,*** and since **Brahman alone is real** in the unreal universe of "*prakruti*", what is unreal cannot be, and never can be its attribute. It is in that sense that Brahman is understood as being "*nirgunan*".

Which of the two interpretations is valid?

2. The Visishtaadvaitin says (per Bhattar's interpretation) that although Brahman is not tainted with the *tri-guna*-s afflicting *prakruti*, it does not mean that the universe is entirely alienated from or unrelated to Brahman who is its ultimate creator.

The Advaitin, on the contrary, avers that since all "*prakruti*" is unreal and Brahman alone is real, the two are definitely unrelated. All *prakruti* is an illusion. There is no question of any contact or relation between the two entities and even less therefore of any question of taint arising to the one from the other. What is *real* can have no truck at all with what is *unreal*.

Which of the two interpretations is valid?

The Unknown Sri Vaishnava began explaining.

****

The conception of Brahman in both schools of Vedanta, the Advaita and Visishtaadvaita, is based solely on the authority (*pramaana*) revealed in the Vedic "*sruti-s*," the Upanishads, and the Brahma-Sutra texts.

When asked the question "*What is Brahman?*" both indeed quote the same "*sruti vaakya*" contained in the famous line of the **Taittireeya Bhruguvalli Upanishad**:

"yatO… vA i…mAni… BUtA†ni… jAya†ntE |

yEna… jAtA†ni… jIva†nti | yat praya†ntya…Bi sam Ævi†Santi |

tad viji†j~jAsasva | tad brahmEti† ||"

("Brughuvalli" – 1.1)

"That from which all these beings are born,

That by which when born they live, and

That unto which when departing,

They enter.

Desire to know verily That:

For that is Brahman!"

Based on the above Upanishad "*vaakya,*" the author of the **Brahma Sutra** (aka *Vedaanta-sutra*), **Rishi Bodhaayana**, defines Brahman as that from which proceed the **Creation**, the **Sustenance,** and the **Dissolution** of the universe (*prakruti*). All the other principal Upanishads (10 out of the 108 said to be extant) therefore describe the Reality of Brahman too in similarly general, all-encompassing – and most often than not, in cryptic, aphoristic terms such as "*sath*", "*Atman*", "*para-tattva*", "*param-jyoti*" etc.

Both the Advaitin and Visishtaadvaitin have no problem in accepting that in accordance with the above "*sruti vaakya,*" Brahman is indeed the Ultimate Reality of their respective school of metaphysics. It is axiomatic truth upon which their respective "*darsana*" or philosophy is founded and developed further. But it is also precisely the point after which they then each begin to follow separate lines or trajectories of thought and hold widely different and dissonant interpretations of the Upanishad "*vaakya.*"

****

For the Visishtaadvaitin, the import of the Upanishad "*vaakya*" is that Brahman is the primary cause of the creation, sustenance, and dissolution of the universe --- "*jagatkaaranatvam"* (Universal Causality) is, therefore, the distinguishing characteristic of the Supreme Being, Brahman. The first two *adhyaayaa*-s or parts of the **Vedanta-Sutra** are devoted in fact to a detailed examination of this important aspect of Brahman as the Ultimate Reality.

By applying the principle of "*jagathkaaranatva,*" the Vedanta-Sutra eliminates all other ontological entities from the purview of the concept of Brahman --- the other entities being individual soul (*jeeva*), primordial cosmic matter (*pradhaana prakruti*), the physical "*aakaasa,*" (ether), the vital airs, '*praana,*' the light of the sun, '*tejas*' etc. which only appear, *prima facie*, to be the **primal causal substance**. Such *elimination* is the seminal or root idea from which the concept of "*suddha-sattva*" of the Visishtaadvaita Vedanta (explained in the previous Dialogue) too got developed.

As S.M.S Chari explains, the *"jagatkaaranatvam" principle* implies that Ultimate Reality, Brahman, **should be** a *sentient being* endowed with *knowledge and power* to create the universe. Brahman, therefore, is *"Purushottaman,"* the *Supreme Personal Being,* the paragon of innumerable attributes of perfection. If as per the Upanishad "*vaakya*," Brahman is that from which all beings are born, by which all beings are sustained and all beings return to terminally, then it is inconceivable that such a Brahman could be utterly *attribute-less* and an *indeterminate* entity. How can the wondrous world that we see around us as Creation --- the mountains, lakes and rainbow skies, the music, poetry, and beauty found in all shapes, hues, and sorts --- be the handiwork of an indeterminate, impersonal ontological entity, devoid of all qualities and totally alienated from all existence, and argued to be non-existent and illusory? *Reductio ad absurdum...!* The Ultimate Reality must therefore be "*saviseshi*" or "*saguna*," a differentiated Being and not "*nirguna*" or "*nirviseshi*."

Student: May I stop you here for just a minute to ask a question seeking a piece of information? Do any of the Upanishads specifically refer to Brahman as "*sagunan*"?

Unknown Sri Vaishnava: We are straying from philosophy now ... and into a question on philology and etymology.... But I concede you do ask an interesting question. If you ask me to quote a specific Upanishad "*vaakya*" where the word "*saguna*" has been employed, I can only ask you to please go on a little expedition on your very own. Please use a suitable online search engine software that can be applied to the entire body of the 108 extant Upanishads that are known to be available. The search hopefully might perhaps throw up some useful results for you.

Please don't think I am being evasive or facetious.

The Sanskrit word "*sagunan*" merely means a paragon "*possessing fulsome attributes*". The **Taittiriya Upanishad (2.7)** uses the synonym "*tenaisha poornah:*" while referring to Brahman as a *Person*, a "*purusha*:" who possesses the quality of all-pervasiveness:

> "*tenaisha poornah:...! Sa va esha purusha vidha eva ....*
> *Tasya purushavidhataam… anvayam purusha vidhah:....*
> *etc."*

And there are in fact several hundreds of similar such Upanishad expressions and passages that can be enumerated as synonyms speaking categorically and variously about attributes that qualify Brahman as a "*sagunan*". Enumerating them is mere statistical exercise… not philosophical inquiry.

Please also remember that I have already brought to your attention the ostensible reason why the word "*sagunan*" is not specifically found in the *Vishnu Sahasranaamam*. (*Dialogue 3*). The same reason could be applied and extended with equal relevance to the Upanishads too in case your software search engine is unable to locate the word in the entire body of those texts.

Student: I understand Sir. Please do proceed from where you left off above.

Unknown Sri Vaishnava: As I was telling you:

The Advaitin's position. Let me summarize it:

Brahman is Ultimate Reality, of course, but it is not the cause of Creation --- **at least not directly** since it is "*nirguna.*" Brahman is one pure, transcendental Consciousness, undifferentiated by any attribute. It is indeterminate, and immutable in character. It is self-evident or self-proved (*svatah-siddham*) and it is self-luminous (*svayam prakaasam*).

Transcendental Consciousness is neither produced nor dissolved – it is "*sath,*" i.e., it just *is* as it always *was* and *will ever be* … It admits of no duality at all.

What the Advaitin means is that no such thing as the universe (*prakruti*) exists anywhere as a separate, existent ontological entity. The plurality of all sentient and insentient beings that is being seen in the universe is a mere illusion created by Perceptive Sense Organs or faculties. It is a product, an apparition of Nescience or "*maayaa*". Once sense-perception ceases, unreality too ceases. What is left then? It is only Consciousness that remains, and that Consciousness (Atma) alone is and continues to be the ultimate reality.

The Advaitin believes therefore none other than Brahman as Pure Consciousness exists. It is purely *subjective cognition with nothing else being the object for itself but itself.* In reality, there can exist only a **Subject,** and never can there be any **Object** qualifying it. It is eternally unchanged and permanent. To conceive or even say then that *Brahman is the primal cause of Creation* etc. would imply that it is an ontological entity that is Subject and what it *creates etc.* immediately becomes Object …. That would be an admission of Duality which goes against the core principle and defining metaphysics of Advaita viz. **Non-duality**.

****

Student: Sir, it baffles me how in the inquiry into the nature (*svarupa*) of Brahman, two entirely dissonant interpretations can be given to the very same Upanishad "*vaakya*"?

Unknown Sri Vaishnava: Indeed, it is! It is one of the axioms of Vedanta Philosophy that the *Word of the Veda* is true, infallible, and consistent within itself. The axiom goes by the technical name in Sanskrit: "***Ekavaakyatvam***." You must understand it to be able to appreciate how fundamental is the difference between the Advaita and Visishtaadvaita positions regarding how to interpret *"sruti vaakya"* or *"pramaana."* Their methods of hermeneutics are so much at variance with each other.

Student: Can you please elaborate?

Unknown Sri Vaishnava: I am going to refer you to a remarkably interesting book which, is in fact, a treasure-house of scriptural references. Do access the book and read it. It is **Sri K.V.Rangaswami Ayyangar's** *"Raja Dharma"* (1941 – Adyar Library). In that book, the doctrine of Vedantic hermeneutics knowns as ***"ekavaakyatvam"*** is explained lucidly. Let me quote it here for your benefit:

QUOTE

*"Absolute unanimity and concord are held to exist between all 'smriti' texts on the same subject and all 'sruti' passages also. The presumption is warranted by the fundamental assumptions of "meemaamsa" (***"saakhaantara-adhikarana"***) that the source of all law, and of all knowledge is the Veda, and that the Veda is eternal, infallible, universal, and derives its authority from itself. It does not recognize any growth in the Veda or any possibility of evolution in Veda or 'smriti.' Homogeneity is a characteristic of the Veda. Self-consistency is its mark. All "veda shaakaa-s" (branches) speak with one voice. This idea is signified as* ***Ekavaakyatvam***.*" The consequences of the presumption are that consistency and harmony must be deemed to exist between one Veda and another, between one passage of 'sruti' and all others, between one 'smriti' and another, between 'sruti' and 'smriti,' as well as between 'smriti' and 'aachaara' (custom, practice, and usage)*

UNQUOTE

Student: "If *"Ekavaakyatvam"* is axiomatic, how to reconcile the Advaitin and the Visishtaadvaitin's diametrically opposed positions regarding the *"nirgunatvam"* of Brahman? Both refer to the same *"sruti vaakya"*! If the *"nirguna"* Brahman of the Advaitin is not the cause of Creation of the universe (*prakruti*), then by whom or by what was the universe that we see around us created – be it real or illusory? The Upanishad "*vaakya*" is categorical when it says, "*That by which when born all beings live, and that unto which when departing, enter.... Etc... yEna... jAtA†ni... jIva†nti | yat praya†ntya...Bi sam Ævi†Santi?*

Unknown Sri Vaishnava: It is a troubling question indeed and made even more troubling because the Advaitin introduces a rather inexplicable cosmic principle or entity called "*avidya*" or "*maaya*" --- meaning, a great veil of Ignorance (call it even *hallucination*!) which envelops all Cognition (*gnyaana*) and utterly impairs if not incapacitates human intelligence from distinguishing between the reality of "*nirguna*" Brahman and that of "*saguna*" Brahman and mistaking the multitudinous, multivarious plurality of "*prakruti*" to be real and virtually blinding it to the reality of the unitary reality behind it all --- which is "*sath*" or "*Brahman*".

The great Acharya of the Advaita school, the venerable pontiff of the **Sankara Mutt,** Kanchipuram, *Pujyashree* **Chandrasekharendra Saraswathi** (1894-1994 CE), in his brilliant commentary on **Adi Sankara's** famous Sanskrit hymn of "*Soundaryalahari*", wrote this while explaining a particular verse therein (Chapter 28 in "*Soundaryalahari*" published by **Bharathi Vidya Bhavan** 2012). It encapsulates the Advaitin position accurately... You must read the book to appreciate Advaita metaphysics.

QUOTE

"The *Nirguna Brahman* of Advaita has no connection whatsoever with *Ishvara*, or the *Saguna Brahman* that conducts the world with the power of *"maaya."* The Nirguna Brahman is by itself and cannot be associated with anything outside of it. **Somehow, and it is a wonder, that no one can explain it.** Maayaa reveals the Nirguna Brahman as the dualistic world. In the dim light of dusk, the rope appears to be a serpent. Has the rope really changed into a serpent? The serpent is an appearance – a phantom – that arises from the rope. But is there, in fact, any connection between the rope and the serpent?"

UNQUOTE

Thus, even for the Advaitin, the concept of *"maaya"* is to quote the Kanchi Acharya, *"somehow a wonder no one can explain…"*!

Student: This concept of *"maaya"* is very befuddling to me, Sir!

Unknown Sri Vaishnava: The introduction of this concept of *"maaya"* into Advaita metaphysics would befuddle every thinking mind. It mystifies me too! But this Advaitin postulation was succinctly explained by the venerable *44th Pontiff of Sri Ahobila Math,* **Sri Vedanta Yathindra Mahaadesikan (Sri Mukkur Azhagiyasingar**) in another one of his lucid epistles. I share it with you here in the hope that *"maaya"* gets de-mystified for you as it did for me:

QUOTE

"*Brahman* that by its very nature is Pure Knowledge (*gnyaana-mayam*) is to be cognized as a being without any attributes. It is *"nirgunam;"* it is eternal; it is all-pervading; there is no other being like it. The reality of this Brahman however is veiled or shrouded by a timeless accompaniment called Ignorance or Avidya (*maaya*). It is Avidya thus which, in effect, produces the hallucinatory world of countless individual souls, of Matter (*prakruti*), of the seas, the mountains, and gods, and makes them all appear as though they were real as if they are true … as in "*tat satyam*."

Whereas, what is real, and the sole absolute reality, is Brahman alone and nothing else i.e., everything that we think we know about the universe to be real -- as "*gnyaatha*," "*gneyam*" and "*gnyaanam*" all in One, or in other words, the *knower*, the *object of knowledge*, and the *knowledge itself* … all three revealed by the Vedas are to be known as mere hallucination ("*mithya*"). This is exactly what is asserted by the followers of this school of philosophy called Advaita.

The unreal individual soul, the "*jivaatma*," through ceaseless contemplation upon its own unreal and non-existent nature, as well as about the unreal world of matter, can eventually rid itself of the veil of Avidya (*maaya*) through *dhyaanam* (meditating upon the real *self* behind the hallucination).

Just as realization finally dawns upon one that the serpent is a mere apparition and it was only the rope, in the first place, which is real and the truth, through "*dhyaanam*" is born "*gnyaana kann*" (the *eye of spiritual realization*) or the enlightenment of the self -- "***aham brahmaasmi***" – through which the unreal soul finally wakes up to the fact "*that my reality is not different from that of Brahman which alone is the true reality, and therefore, I too am that Brahman alone and there is really nothing else*". That "*gnyaana*" itself is what constitutes '***moksham***' or Salvation for the Advaitin. To say, however, that the individual soul in that state of "*moksha*" also separately experiences the Bliss of Brahman in some other separate plane of reality called, say, **Vaikuntam** is false.

"This philosophical position is what is called **Advaita** and its followers interpret the revealed truths of Vedanta metaphysics in this way.

UNQUOTE

Student: So what you have just now explained is that *maaya* is *avidya* or ignorance or nescience ... and it is that which leads us to see plurality (i.e. *the metaphoric snake*) instead of the reality (*the metaphoric rope*)? So, can we not say then that *maaya* seems to be quite a plausible Vedantic concept after all?

Unknown Sri Vaishnava: We must be very careful about Vedantic semantics here ... especially since we are engaging ourselves with English translations of the word "*maaya*" and "*avidya*". The two are not really synonymous.

The Advaitin used the term "*maaya*" to denote a metaphoric and metaphysical **Veil** that separates that which alone is Real (*Brahman*) from everything else Unreal. It is the great phenomenal *Veil* that makes the *unreal,* the *non-existent,* and the *untrue* (i.e.the snake) appear as though it is *real, existent,* and *true (i.e.*the rope*).*

The Visishtaadvaitin uses the term "*avidya*" in an entirely different and distinct sense. He uses it to denote *Ignorance* born of **Karma** which deludes the *Atma*, the soul, into thinking that it is an independent *("svaatantryam")* ontological entity existing separately from Brahman. Such "*svaantatrayam*" is born of **free will** which sees itself as being autonomous from the divine will... and that in itself is but the result of *Karma*. Karma is thus the most critical element in the conception of *Avidya* in the Visishtaadvaitic sense.

Student: Does the Advaitin cite any clear and incontrovertible "*sruti vaakya*" that establishes this strange, inexplicable notion of "*maaya*" or "*mithyaa*"?

Unknown Sri Vaishnava: According to the Visishtaadvaitin, the concept of "*maayaa*" is wholly un-Vedantic.

Student: If that is so, then where did the Advaitin source the concept? From where did it originate? Surely, not out of imagination or thin air?!

Unknown Sri Vaishnava: Visishtaadvaitins call the Advaita metaphysics of "*nirguna brahman*" by a curious name: "*pracchanna boudheyam*" which translates into "***Crypto-Buddhism.***" In his work titled "***siddha-traya,***" the Vaishnava philosopher and the predecessor of Sri Ramanuja, **Sri Yaamunachaarya (917-1042 CE)** stated that Buddhism and Advaita metaphysics that is centered on "*maayaavada*", were the same thing. The only difference he could see was that while one was openly Buddhist – "*prakata saugata*" – the other was simply Buddhism disguised as Vedanta – "*pracchannna saugata.*"

So, to answer your question, the concept of Advaitic "*maayaa*" has its origins in Buddhist thought which the Advaitins who came much after Adi Sankara relied upon far too heavily to develop it into the cornerstone of their school of metaphysics.

Student: On what basis do you say that Sir? My understanding is that the *rope/snake* allegory which explains the concept of *avidya* or *maya* (distortion brought about by the perception of sense organs and the mind) is cited even in the **Mundaka Upanishad**. If so, it clearly predates Buddhism by a few thousand years. Then how would it be correct to say that it was *borrowed from Buddhism*?

Unknown Sri Vaishnava: Please go to the original text of the *Mundaka Upanishad*. There is no mention there at all of the "*snake/rope*" allegory. Someone seems to have misled you. So, please do not unduly confuse yourself with dates and periods.

Be that as it may, without seeming to suggest that Advaita borrowed from Buddhist school of thought, let me say this: Advaita as first propounded by Sri Adi Sankara in the 8th century evolved and branched out further into many subschools for hundreds of years in the Post-Sankara period. When the Visishtaadvaitin refers to "*praccanna saugata*" he is possibly referring only in a general sort of way to the many variant schools of *Post-Sankara Advaitic thought* which seemingly bordered on or closely resembled, even if they did not in any way directly borrow from the Buddhist's metaphysics. The term "*borrowing*" should not therefore be regarded as derogatory in any sense at all in this context.

Student: Again, on what basis do you say all this, Sir?

Unknown Sri Vaishnava: If you were to understand the historical background of Advaita and how it emerged in India during the time of **Sri Adi Sankara Bhagavathpaada** you will concur with me.

In his book **"Indian Philosophy,"** II, pp-470-473 and 496-497, **Dr. S. Radhakrishnan** points out why Advaita is seen to be resembling certain elements (please underline "*certain elements*") in Buddhistic schools of thought:

QUOTE

"It is said, not without truth, that Brahmanism ('purva-meemaamsa') killed Buddhism (in India) silently assimilating many Buddhist practices, condemned animal sacrifice, accepted Buddha as an avatar of Vishnu, and thus absorbed the best elements of the Buddhist faith. (Later) ... Buddhism created a region of thought ... in the life of the country ... a certain atmosphere from which no mind could escape, and it undoubtedly exercised a far-reaching influence on Sankara's mind.

"An Indian tradition opposed to Sankara holds that he is a Buddhist in disguise and his 'maaya-vaada' but crypto-Buddhism....

Vignyaana-bhikshu *(1550-1600 CE) observes: "There is not a single "brahma-sutra" in which our bondage is declared to be due to mere ignorance (or illusion). As to the novel theory of 'maaya' propounded by persons calling* *themselves Vedantists, it is only a species of the subjective idealism of the Buddhists. The theory is not a tenet of the Vedanta...."*

"These (such) estimates imply that Sankara incorporated certain Buddhist elements such as the doctrine of "maaya" and monasticism into the Vedanta philosophy."

Student: I find it remarkably interesting, Sir, that Dr. Radhakrishnan, an eminent exponent of Advaita Vedanta himself, refers to Advaita as *Crypto-Buddhism*.

Unknown Sri Vaishnava: Both Advaita and Buddhism are great systems of philosophical thought in our country. Therefore, please do not fall into the trap of thinking that the term *"crypto-Buddhism"* is in any way an uncharitable or undignified characterization of Advaita. It only serves as a convenient albeit awkward or inelegant *label* -- that's all. It carries no offensive connotation. You will understand it when you read what Sri K.V. Rangaswami Aiyangar (in the same book *"Rajadharma"* I referred you to earlier) comments on the above observations of Dr. Radhakrishnan…. He writes as follows:

QUOTE

"In a sense, it may therefore be said that Sankara stole the Buddhist's thunder. That the "borrowing" is perhaps not direct but due to both Buddhist and Advaitic thought, being directly descended from the thought of the Upanishads does not alter the effect on the displacement of Buddhists by the neo-Brahminical i.e Vedantic thought. The personal orthodoxy of Sankara will have given a point to the change. (But) there are similarities between the views of Buddhism and the Advaita Vedanta.

"The Buddha had meanwhile been accepted as an avatar of Vishnu. In some traditions, he takes the place of 'Isvara' (i.e., Shiva) who is made to say (in the 'Padmapuraana' Uttarakhaanda, ch.236) that in the Kaliyuga he would himself declare the 'maayaavaada' to be false doctrine. The implication of the acceptance of the Buddha as an avatar of Vishnu is that he appears as the champion of Vedic Dharma. That there is no incongruity in the legend will be manifest to those who remember that the Buddha lived and died a Hindu and that the belief that he was opposed to the Vedas is not correct."

UNQUOTE

Unknown Sri Vaishnava: It is ironic that in the history of Indian Philosophy, the Buddhist system of thought was regarded by both the Advaita and Visishtaadvaita schools of Vedanta as fundamentally atheistic and un-Vedantic since it had no place in its metaphysics for an entity such as *Brahman, Atma, Guna, Suddha-Satvam*, etc. in it... But then for the dyed-in-wool adherent of the Visishtaadvaita school of Vedanta, the line between Advaita and Crypto-Buddhism has been always only a very thin one.

Student: Sir, you quote K.V.Rangaswami Aiyangar as saying that *"there are similarities between the views of Buddhism and the Advaita Vedanta."* Can you point me out to a few specific examples?

Unknown Sri Vaishnava: I certainly can but they would not be germane to the core subject of ***Nirgunatvam*** which we are discussing. You must understand that the Buddhist wholly rejects Vedic/Vedantic metaphysics whereas Advaita is firmly rooted in it. The two schools therefore would have nothing really to say to each other about *Nirgunatvam*. If we go into that subject now, we will only be digressing from the main theme of our dialogue.

Student: Nonetheless, sir, please very briefly do explain to me where do the two schools stand on matters related to Brahman, especially with respect to Consciousness.

****

Dialogue 6

A Brief Digression into Post-Sankara Buddhism

Student: Sir, very briefly please do explain to me where do the two schools, Advaita and Buddhism, stand on matters related to Brahman, especially with respect to Consciousness. After all, both the Advaitin and the Buddhist do posit *Consciousness*, don't they? And both do have a conception of cosmic genesis too... *"jagath-kaaranam"*, don't they? Please can you shed a bit of light just to whet my curiosity about the similarities and dissimilarities?

Unknown Sri Vaishnava: I refer you to a book titled **"WHAT THE BUDDHA TAUGHT"** written by a pre-eminent Buddhist scholar in 1959, **Walpola Rahula** *(refer Bibliography)*. He was recognized in the Buddhist community then as ***"Tripitika-vaageeshwara-acharya"***: *"Supreme Master of Buddhist Scriptures"*. You must read his book. From the book one can easily glean the few examples you seek of *"similarities between the views of Buddhism and the Advaita Vedanta on the nature of Consciousness."* But let me cite just one or two for your benefit.

As you know Buddhism denies the existence of the ***Atma***, whether it is the individual soul of *"jeevaatma"* or the Supreme Soul, *"paramaatma."* The Buddhist also rejects the idea of *"Ultimate and Un-caused Cause"* of the Universe (*prakruti*) or *"jagatkaaranatvam."*

Now, let me quote to you a few passages on these two specific tenets from the book "*What the Buddha Taught*":

QUOTE:

(i) "What in general is suggested by the Soul, Self, Ego, or to use the Sanskrit expression, Atman, is that in man there is a permanent, everlasting, and absolute entity, which is unchanging substance behind the changing phenomenal world. According to some religions, each individual has such a separate soul which is created by God, and which, finally, after death, lives eternally either in hell or heaven, its destiny depending on the judgment of its creator. According to others, it goes through many lives till it is completely purified and becomes finally united with God or Brahman., Universal Soul, or (param) Atman, from which is originally emanated. This soul or self in man is the thinker of thoughts, feeler of sensations, and receiver of rewards and punishments for all its actions, good and bad. Such a conception is called the idea of self.

(ii) Buddhism stands unique in the history of human thought in denying the existence of such a Soul, or Atman. According to the teachings of the Buddha, the idea of self is an imaginary, false belief that has no corresponding reality, and it produces harmful thoughts of "me" and "mine,' selfish desires, craving, attachment, hatred, ill-will, conceit, pride, egoism, and other defilements, impurities, and problems. It is the source of all the troubles in the world from personal conflicts to wars between nations. In short, to this false view can be traced all the evil in the world.

(iii) The doctrine of No-Soul in Buddhism is called "anatta" and it is the natural result of, or the corollary to the Buddha's teaching of a doctrine called "patticcha-samuppaada," which is translated as "Conditioned Genesis." According to this doctrine, nothing in this world is absolute. Everything is conditioned, relative and interdependent. It is the Buddhist theory of relativity. On this principle of conditionality, relativity, and inter-dependence, the whole existence and continuity of life and its cessation

too are explained. No first cause of the universe is accepted by Buddhism.

(iv) According to the doctrine of Conditioned Genesis, the idea of an abiding, immortal substance in man or outside, whether it is called Atman, I, Soul, Self of Ego, is considered only a false belief, a mere mental projection.

(v) When we use such expressions in our daily life as 'I,' 'you,' 'being,' 'individual,' etc. we do not lie because there is no self or being as such, but we speak a truth which is confirming to the convention of the world. But the ultimate truth is that there is no 'I,' or 'being.'

(vi) The negation of an imperishable Atman is the common characteristic of all dogmatic systems of the Lesser as well as the Great Vehicle, and there is, therefore, no reason to assume that Buddhist tradition which is in complete agreement on this point has deviated from the Buddha's original teaching.

UNQUOTE

Unknown Sri Vaishnava: From a reading of the above six passages, you can easily see the startling similarities between the Buddhist view of **Atman** and the Advaitic view of **Atman**. The Advaitin does not deny the existence of Atman while the Buddhist does so. But then the Advaitin and the Buddhist do both agree in principle that the Atman is "*mere mental projection*" produced by nescience and that "*the ultimate truth is that there is no 'I,' or 'being' in reality*". (Vide passages *(iv)* and *(v)* above).

Besides, as you can see, the Buddhist himself recognizes the congruence of his position with that of Advaita philosophy when he says (in the passage *(vi)* above) that "t*he negation of an imperishable Atman is the common characteristic of all dogmatic systems of the Lesser as well as the Great Vehicle....*"! We must also not fail to notice that the expression "*dogmatic systems of the Lesser as well as the*

Great Vehicle..." used in the passage was, a thinly veiled reference to the Advaitic notion of *"higher Nirguna Brahman"* and *"lower Saguna Brahman"*.

The Buddhist rejection of *"jagatkaaranatvam"* is, one might say, only a more **rational-sounding** (and not necessarily *rational*) alternative to -- and a more developed version of -- the Advaitin's own fundamental tenet that the Universe, *"prakruti"*, was not created by Brahman but has been only brought about by a great cosmic power of Nescience called *"maayaa"* i.e., the *mental projection of unreality* as suggested in the famous metaphor of the rope and the serpent.

Student: What do you mean, Sir, when you say, *"more rational-sounding"* alternative to the Advaitin's own tenet"?!

Unknown Sri Vaishnava: I say that because the Advaitin attributes the creation of the universe to the inexplicable, inscrutable cause of *"maaya shakthi"* – a power of nescience that he himself can neither fathom nor unravel – the Kanchi Acharya himself called it *"a wonder that no one can explain"*! Whereas the Buddhist while positing the same nescience is, however, able to rationalize it and theorize about how it came about.

All creation for the Buddhist arises in Nescience... and when asked how Nescience or *"maayaa"* itself is created, he offers us a theory he claims is **rational**. He calls it the doctrine of *"Conditioned Genesis"* .... *"patticcha-samuppaada"* (a Pali term) according to which the cause of the universe or "*prakruti*" lies in infinite progress and/or regress of relative conditions of existence that, in turn, are perennially getting configured and re-configured because of deeds and choices that Buddhism describes as "*volitional action*", in other words, **karma**.

Student: But why do you characterize the theory to be *rational-sounding...* or simply, rationalisation?

Unknown Sri Vaishnava: Once again let me quote Walpola Rahula, the Buddhist Master, from his book and you will understand why.

QUOTE:

The doctrine of *Conditioned Genesis* is a formula that explains Buddha's view of universal causality through a 12-step process:

1. Through ignorance are conditioned volitional actions or "karma-formations".

2. Through volitional actions is conditioned consciousness.

3. Through consciousness are conditioned mental and physical phenomena.

4. Through mental and physical phenomena are conditioned the 6 faculties (5 sense organs and the mind).

5. Through the 6 faculties is conditioned sensorial and mental contact with the universe (or "prakruti").

6. Through contact with the universe is conditioned sensation ("vedanaa")

7. Through sensation is conditioned Desire, thirst.

8. Through Desire (thirst) is conditioned clinging.

9. Through clinging is conditioned the process of becoming.

10. Through the process of becoming is conditioned birth.

11. Through birth is conditioned again ignorance

12. And through ignorance is conditioned the 12 states of dukkha ---- aging, disease, decay, death, pain, lamentation ... etc.

This is how life arises, exists, and continues. If we take this formula in reverse order, we come to the cessation of the process viz.:

Through the cessation of ignorance, volitional activities, or karma-formation ceases; through the cessation of volitional activities, consciousness ceases.... through the cessation of birth, *dukka* ceases.... (And the cessation of all *dukkha* is Buddhist "*nirvaana*", the emptying of all existential conditionality). It should be remembered that each of the above factors or steps is conditioned as well as conditioning... *Conditioned Genesis* should be considered as a circle, and not as a chain."

UNQUOTE

****

Student: Incidentally, Sir, I wish to put this to you in a lighter vein. Considering that Advaitic thought as found in the Upanishads predates Buddhism, I thought calling Buddhism "**Crypto-Advaita**" would be more appropriate?

Unknown Sri Vaishnava: *Ha! Ha! What an original thought*! Indeed, the Advaitin would certainly endorse your statement!

Student: Sir, please can you permit me to digress a little here at this point in our discussions?

Unknown Sri Vaishnava: No problem. As it is, aren't we engaged in a long digression already now? ....Go ahead.

Student: Did not Adi Sankara himself compose so many wonderful hymns in praise and worship of the wondrous "*kalyaana guna-s*" and attributes of "*saguna*" deities like *Shiva, Devi, Amba, Vishnu, and Narasimha*? Did he not compose them all in the true spirit of ***Bhakthi*** which is a valid Vedantic *upaaya* for both Advaitin and Visishtaadvaitin, after all? Even though ultimately Sankara upholds the Advaitic idea of Brahman as "*nirviseshi*" and "*nirgunanan*" only – and he affirms the theory of "*maaya*" and that of the world being mere "*mithyaa*" too -- does he not at the same time sing the glories of Godhead much like the Visishtaadvaitin does about the "*kalyaana guna-ganaan*" and that too in such scintillating Sanskrit poetic *stotras* like the famous "*Bhaja Govindam*", "*Soundarya Lahari*", "*Manthraraaja-pada Stotram*", "*Lakshmi-Narasimha Karaavalamba stotram*" etc.? Did Sankara also not write brilliant expositions and commentaries on *smriti*-texts such as *the Vishnu Sahasranaamam, Lalita Sahasranaamam,* and the *Bhagavath-Gita* which are all essentially works affirming and celebrating the "*saguna*" qualities of the Upanishad Brahman"?

Unknown Sri Vaishnava: What you say is true.

Student: In the theological sense, if not in the philosophical, and in terms of spiritual "*saadhana*" or effort too, aren't Advaitin and Visishtaadvaitin having so much in common? Why then cannot both Vedantic schools thus accept both are fellow travelers pursuing the very same course of spiritual quest and are aiming to reach the same destination too?

Unknown Sri Vaishnava: I am glad you ask me this question. Like you, many people ask why both schools of Vedanta go about making so much of a fuss over the philosophical issue of Nirgunatvam? *Why can't they get along? "Who really cares about it, after all?!"* they ask!

Such popular ("*progressive*") thinking amongst the common people, which is dismissive, if not disdainful of the fundamental issue between the two Vedanta-schools, has for long persisted, in fact, within my own mind too. I too began to believe that the age-old hermeneutical spat on the matter of "*nirguna Brahman*" between Advaitin and Visishtaadvaitin is one that only rabbinical-minded members within both sects worry about. For ordinary laity in both communities, it is best to completely ignore it… to shove the elephant in the living room firmly under the carpet, so to say, and move on in life. But then we must accept that *Philosophy is Philosophy*…. and genuine philosophers cannot and will never budge from their convictions.

Student: And you, Sir, do you agree with that common and popular viewpoint? Or, with the philosophers who will not budge from conviction?

Unknown Sri Vaishnava: Whenever I engage with friends and students like you, belonging to either Advaita and Visishtaadvaita '*darsana*-s,' I find that many of them hardly know much about the fundamental differences between "*saguna*" and "*nirguna*" conception of the Upanishadic Brahman. Even many Sri Vaishnavites, young and old these days, are not acquainted at all with the subject matter of Vedanta Desikan's "*satadushani*." And even if they were indeed vaguely aware of such differences, they tend to simply ignore and overlook them all since, personally, they have been somehow let to believe that "*it does not really matter at all*"!

Student: So, tell me, Sir, *does it matter to you*, or *does it not matter*?

Unknown Sri Vaishnava: It is exceedingly difficult for me to give you a very straightforward answer to such a direct question. But then let me put it this way….

I am not a philosophy-scholar, and very much like you, dear young man, I too am just a lifelong student of Vedanta. My interest in it was first kindled many years ago by my "*maanaseeka guru,*" "***vaikunta vaasi,*** " **U.Ve. Sri Mukkur Lakshminarasimhachariar.** Seated at his feet, I had been able to learn and grasp elementary aspects of the various tenets, nuances, and shades of differences between Advaita and Visishtaadvaita philosophies about the **Nirgunatvam** of Brahman spoken in the Upanishads.

Learning expands the mind, writing distills it. And dialogues like these that we are having now truly crystallize it!

While I am talking to you now on this subject, I am also at the same time, *reprocessing, distilling*, and *crystallizing* within my mind much of what I had learned about "*nirgunatvam*" from my "*guru*" many years ago.

For many years after my guru passed away, as part of my continuous self-education in philosophical subjects, I have been reading a lot on Vedanta, as well as listening to lectures and discourses of many other eminent *vidwaans* and *vedadhyaayees* on the question of *Nirgunatvam*. All that self-learning has only made me deeply aware of the fact -- and let me say I am extremely surprised by it too -- that in the eyes of the public as well as within academic and learned circles, both within India and abroad, it is Advaita metaphysics and epistemology alone that has become representative of Vedanta. It is Advaita that rules the roost even in Western academia.

Even as I am explaining to you in these conversations of ours, I must tell you that in so far as the matter of "*nirgunatvam*" is concerned --- and I underline it, *only* in so far as the "*nirgunatva*" question is concerned --- what Advaita posits is not really Vedanta at all; it is *"pracchanna baudheyam"* or crypto-Buddhism.

Anytime an Advaitin seeks to make the specious distinction between **Brahman-real** and **Brahman-crypto** --- i.e. *nirguna* and *saguna Brahman* respectively --- he is espousing only "*pracchanna baudheyam*". Now, that position of Advaita to me is unacceptable for the simple reason that it renders the whole of Advaitin metaphysics to be neither here nor there… and I daresay, a bit woolly-headed even.

Student: What do you mean, Sir?

Unknown Sri Vaishnava: Again, I must give you an indirect answer and let you figure out for yourself the real substance of what I am saying.

Many a stalwart Advaita Acharya has written very many illuminating commentaries and delivered marvelous commentaries on the magnificent works of Adi Sankara, who is the acknowledged founder of the Advaita Vedanta School in India. When you study those **post-Sankara** commentaries and discourses on the Sanskrit hymns and literature of Adi Sankara which Advaitin-followers wrote, and when you read *between the lines*, as it were, you will not fail to observe them, here and there but ever so often, invariably straying away from their main position and cardinal purport in the strictest monistic interpretation of texts. You will find them unwittingly, and unconsciously, slipping into engaging in *saguna Brahman* discourse only even while expounding Advaitic thought and principles of *nirgunatvam*. Which is indeed really *neither here nor there…*

One can easily sense in such works the strain the Advaita exponents undergo in having to belabor contrived logic just to be able to *reconcile the irreconcilable*…. i.e., to defend *Nirgunatvam* against *Sagunatvam*, *Maaya* against *jagatkaaranatvam*, and trying to reconcile the ontological reality of *Prakruthi* with the unreality of *nescience*.

The Advaitin's effort in such hermeneutics, many a time to the reader, would appear as though it were only trying to square circles … or, hammering in square pegs into round holes.

Of course, today an inveterate Advaitin will never concede that Advaita hermeneutics does often seem to end up tying itself in all sorts of knots while trying to read "*nirgunatvam*" into scriptural texts and denying "*sagunatvam*" even in the face of overwhelming scriptural evidence found in them in its favor.

But then, objectively speaking, the Advaitin conviction cannot altogether be said to carry little weight. The great seer and Advaita Acharya of *the Kamakoti Mutt at Kanchi*, Sri Chandrasekharendra Saraswati, explained the situation masterfully while giving his commentary on the "*Saundaryalahari*" (*Chapter 3, Page 7 & 8*):

QUOTE:

"If you ask how a *gnyaani* who remains an Advaitin inwardly seems (however) to function as a Dvaitin (dualist) outwardly, we can reply only by saying that it is all part of the divine sport."

"Even if he has been freed of his mind and of *Maaya*, it does not mean that the outward world and with it the cosmos of living creatures have become extinct. What does this show?

"It is a Great Mind that has created all this, and at the same time, it is the same Great Mind that helps people under the sway of *Maaya*, letting them act according to their whims. It is this power that the monistic (Advaita) system calls *Saguna Brahman*, **Isvara**. In the *Saakta* and *Saiva* systems, it is called *Sakthi*, *Paraashakthi*, *Amba*, while the *Nirguna Brahman* is called **Sivam**. Just as the Nirguna Brahman functions as the Saguna Brahman in the outward world of *karma*, the *gnyaani* who has achieved perfection in his experience of the Nirguna Brahman is kept engaged in the outward world (*prakruti*) by the Saguna Brahman."

UNQUOTE

Student: You touched upon the contradiction between Sri Sankara's **bhakti** element (as witnessed in his compositions) and his concept of the Nirguna Brahman. My understanding is that Advaita Vedanta provides for calibrated evolution on the path to Self-Realisation, and that *bhakti* has a role to play in bringing about "*chitta shudhi*" (purification of consciousness) which is a fundamental pre-requisite for attaining *Brahma gnyaana*. As the seeker advances in his spiritual journey, he may not need some of those *bhakthi*-related supports or props …. Somewhat like a pole-vaulter letting go of the pole once he is at the zenith of his take-off trajectory.

Unknown Sri Vaishnava: Good point you make… and once again it is the great Kanchi Acharya who explained it masterfully:

QUOTE

"There is an erroneous belief that the goal of **Bhakthi** is to become separated from the Lord and to worship him in an attitude of dualism. That is why people ask how a *gnyaani* (a non-dualist Advaitin) can follow (both) the path of devotion and Advaita (at the same time). They are not aware of the fact that even in such bhakthi as in which the Lord and the devotee are separate entities, the latter will eventually be taken to the state in which he will be able to pray thus: **"Without ever being separated from you, Lord, I must become one with you."** When he reaches such a state, the *"Kaarya Brahman"* or the Saguna Brahman that is *Paraashakthi* will bless him with the *gnyaana* that will take him to the monistic entity called *"Kaaraana Brahman"* or the Nirguna Brahman."

UNQUOTE

Unknown Sri Vaishnava: However, let this be clear. Advaita metaphysics positing the idea of *"lower saguna Brahman"* and *"a higher nirguna brahman"* was severely criticized by **Paraashara Bhattar** in the eloquent preamble to the *"Bhagavath Guna Darpana"* which he wrote as commentary to the Vishnu Sahasranaama:

> *"sagunaa nirgunaartheti maa cha vaa chaala! vochathaah: I*
>
> *Na virudhaartha-yor-yasmaath upayo-peyathaa dvayoh: II"*

Oh, prattler! Do not argue that of the two viz. of the worship of God with attributes and of God without attributes, the former is a step towards the latter. For the two are contradictory to each other and one cannot be a step to lead to the other.

Bhattar then put forth a formidable argument against the concept of *"two Brahmans"* propounded by the Advaitin:

QUOTE

"If the teaching of yours be true – that Brahman with attributes is for persons who are entitled to a lesser objective other than *"moksha"* or salvation, and that the Brahman without attributes alone is indeed for those who aspire for it" --- then I say, *"Fie unto you! Your ears are surely deaf!"*

You do not seem to hear what has been said in the *Sahasranaamam* itself to be the fruits of reciting the *"naama-s"*! It is loudly proclaimed in this very *stotra* towards the end (in the *phala sruti* passages) as follows:

"…. muchyate janma samsara bandhanaath…." i.e., *"release from the bonds of samsara…"* and,

"…. yaathi brahma sanaatanam…."

i.e., "attaining the eternal Brahman…."

"If you once postulate two Brahmans, one with and the other without attributes, the one-ness of the Brahman which you yourself advocate will be destroyed.

"At the beginning of the *Sahasranaamam*, to the question, *"What is the best means, or Dharma, by which Salvation is attained?"* the answer given is the same i.e., worship of Brahman of countless perfect attributes i.e.

"ko dharmah sarva dharmaanaam, bhavatah paramo mathah"? **is the question posed by Yudhishtira to Bheeshmaaachaarya whose categorical answer then is** *"…esha me sarva dharmaanaam dharmo adhika-tamo mathah…."*

If you say that even then it is only the lesser Brahman that is being mentioned, where else will there be an opportunity to reach the highest One?!"

UNQUOTE

Unknown Sri Vaishnava: Therefore, young man, to your question whether it matters to me, or does not matter to me at all, that there is truly little to choose between the Advaita and Visishtaadvaita positions on "*nirgunatvam*" of Brahman .... Well, my answer is, of course, *it does matter a lot to me...* It matters to me as much that as chalk and cheese, although they may *look* very alike to me, they can never really, however, *be* the same to me.

****

Dialogue 7

Ramanuja "*darsana*": "*Jagath-Kaaranatvam*" And "*Apprthak-Siddhi*"

Student: Sir, two specific questions previously raised only in the passing (Dialogue 5 and 6) should now be examined more closely. They are inter-related and inter-linked, hence can be discussed jointly.

1. What is the polemics between the Advaita and Visishtaadvaita schools of Vedanta on the issue of whether Brahman is without Guna or abounds in Gunas?

2. The Visishtaadvaitin says (per Paraashara Bhattar's interpretation) that "although Brahman is not tainted with the tri-guna-s afflicting prakruti, he nonetheless remains in eternal contact with the entire universe (prakruti)....". The Advaitin, on the contrary, avers that since all "prakruti" is unreal and Brahman alone is real, there is no question of any contact between the two entities and even much less, therefore, of any question of taint arising therefrom.

Which of the two interpretations is valid?

Unknown Sri Vaishnava: **Question no. 2** above being easier to answer than the first, it is being taken up first for examining. Let us address **Question no.1** later.

****

As far as the Advaitin is concerned, the whole question of "*guna*" is irrelevant. Be it "*triguna*" or "*suddha-sattva*," "*bhagavath-guna*" or "*visesha*" or "*vaibhava*" etc. they are all rejected outright since, according to him, all except Brahman is unreal and mere illusion (*maaya or mithyaa*). Hence it would be pointless to argue further with the Advaitin on that score. In the Advaita school, "*prakruti*" is an unreal entity and so there is no such thing as any relationship with the reality of Brahman.... **Period.**

The question, therefore, is to be addressed only to the Visishtaadvaitin, and it is he who must answer the following:

How can "*prakruthi*" ever bear any conceivable relation to Brahman? How can both "*bhagavath-guna*" and "*triguna*" coexist and correlate in the universe? How is it logical to say that what is, by nature, impermanent (*asath*) is also however, at the very same time, a part of what is eternal (*sath*), and yet the two are distinct and never the twain do meet?! *How paradoxical*!

How tenable is the view that Brahman who according to you, is all "*suddha-sattva*," the paragon of auspicious "*kalyaana-guna*" and perfections, remains unconditioned by and yet remains ever related at the same time to *prakruti* -- i.e., the universe of *cit* and *acit*, *sentient* beings and *insentient* matter -- with all its inherent imperfections, infirmities, and impermanence (*vikaaram*)? Or in other words, how does Brahman remain untouched and unaffected by the "*tri-gunas*" of *sattva*, *rajas,* and *tamas?*

****

The Visishtaadvaitin's answer to the questions is paraphrased below.

Bhagavath Sri Ramanujachaarya

There are a pair of twin-ontological principles underpinning the Visishtaadvaitin's position that "*although Brahman is not tainted with the tri-guna-s afflicting prakruti, he nonetheless remains eternally and inseparably related with the entire universe (prakruti)....*" They are:

1. *"jagatkaaranatvam"* and *"upaadaana-kaaranatvam"*
2. *"apprthak-siddhi"* and *"sarira-sariri-bhaavam"*

Each of the above principles is very briefly enunciated below:

"*jagatkaaranatvam*"

- The fact that Brahman is the primal cause of substance of the universe (*jagatkaarana*) implies that it should also be a sentient being (*chetana vastu*) endowed with omniscience and omnipotence, as otherwise the creation of an orderly, beautiful, and awe-inspiring universe would be logically inconceivable.

- The Brahman causes the universe by pure **Will** ... i.e., "*sankalpa*." The Chandogya Upanishad attests to this *(VI.2.1)*:

"*sadeva somyedam-agra-aaseedekamevaadviteeyam... tadaikshata bahusyaam prajaayaayeti; tattejo ashrjata....*"

"In the beginning, my dear, this was Being alone (sadeva), one only, without a second'... The Being willed, "May I become many," "may I grow forth," "it created fire... etc."

- The attribution of the **Will** (*bhagavath-sankalpa* or "*Ikshana*") to Brahman implies that the metaphysical Reality must be a sentient being endowed with *knowledge* and *power* to create the universe. Ramanuja, therefore, asserts that Brahman is "*purushottama*," the Supreme Personal Being qualified with numerous attributes. In his **Bhaashya** (commentary) to the *Vedanta-sutra* (I.1.1), he says this:

"*brahamasabdena cha svabhaavato nirasta-nikhila-doshaha-anavadhi-katishyaasankhyeya-kalyaana-guna-ganaah-purushottamo abhidheeyathe....*"

This would mean that Reality is "*savisesha*"/*saguna*," a differentiated Being and *not* "*nirvisesha*," a transcendental undifferentiated Being as the Advaitin maintains. Such an

Advaitic type of Reality cannot have a *causal relationship* with the universe and cannot have any bearing with *"prakruti"* either. It will be as good as a non-effectual non-entity.

The Advaitin, of course, on the other hand, does try to get over the difficulty by postulating, as we saw earlier, the theory of a *"saguna brahman'* being another entity that is *lower* than *the "higher nirguna brahman."* He then endows the *'lower Brahman'* with all the attributes such as *"saguna," "savisesha,"* omnipotence and omniscience which the Visishtaadvaitin attributes to the only one Brahman that exists who is the *"jagatkaaranan"* ... But the Advaitin will not give up the postulate that the *'lower Saguna Brahman'* is *"maaya* or *mithyaa,"* an illusory manifestation distinct from the ultimate Brahman which alone is the Ultimate *nirguna/nirvisesha* Reality.

The ambivalence and equivocation of the Advaitin's position vis-à-vis "guna" and "jagathkaaranatvam" stand exposed in the way in which -- in the 90th *shloka* of Sri Vishnu Sahasranaamam, (i.e., **"Anur Brihat Krishas Sthulo Gunabhrin Nirguno Mahaan |Adhritah Svadhritas Svaasyah Praagvamsho Vamshavardhanah II"**) -- the Sankara *"bhaashya"* interprets the 839th *"naama"* in it viz. **"gunabhrin"**:

- In the *"Sankara-bhaashya"* there is the hint of a tacit admission, in fact, that this *"naama"* of *"gunabrhrin"* denotes *"jagathkaaranatvam."* For the explanation given for the *"naama"* is that it means **(Quote)** *"the support of the "guna-s." He is so-called because, in the creative cycle of creation, sustentation, and dissolution, Brahman is the support of the three "guna-s" – "sattva, rajas and tamas" – with which those functions are performed."* **(Unquote)**. But then immediately thereafter, while interpreting the ensuing *"naama," "nirguna"* (discussed in Dialogue 4), the *"Sankara-bhaashya"* adds a strange interjectory line of disclaimer!

viz.: ... **"As the "*guna*-s" are unreal metaphysically, Brahman is "*nirguna*".**

Thus, after reading the above, we are left asking incredulously:

"To which entity does the *"naama" of "gunabhrin"* then denote? The Advaitin's *lower "saguna Brahman"? The Brahman who is unreal? Or the "nirguna Brahman" who alone is real?! Are we then to believe that the real is supported by the unreal?!"*

Thus, there is really no way out of the illogical corner into which the Advaitin with his interpretation thus paints himself into.

****

- Paraashara Bhattar's interpretation, on the other hand, of the name "*gunabhrin*" is simple and unambiguous. In fact, his interpretation clearly establishes the link between the "*gunas*" and the "*jagatkaaranatvam*":

QUOTE

*"With his own Will (sankalpa), He sustains the entire universe in all its states (i.e., of creation, sustentation, and dissolution) and supports it. This is described by this name. This is his preeminence and splendor. "**sarvasya vashi sarvasya eeshaanah**" (Brihadaaranyaka Upanishad, 6-4-22) ...*

UNQUOTE

It must be noted that the Upanishad word "*eeshaana*," meaning "*controllership*" or "*overlordship*" is synonymous with the word "*ikshana*" (Will) referred to above, meaning *oversight, care, and superintendence* .... And they are thus both defining attributes of "*jagathkaaranatvam*" and "*bhagavath-sankalpam*."

<u>**"*Upaadaana kaaranatvam*":**</u>

The English translation of this Sanskrit expression is "*material cause*" and it is also one of the connotations of "*gunabhrin.*" S.M.S. Chari explains this principle very well as follows:

QUOTE

- "According to the theory of causality (i.e., Cause and Effect) accepted by Visishtaadvaita, the *Effect* is the modified state of the *Cause* and the two are non-distinct in the sense that the causal substance is immanent in the effected products.

- "Brahman, as the Primary Cause of the universe, establishes the fact it is the ground or "*aadhaara*" of the universe of all sentient and insentient beings in it (*cit* and *acit*). The **Chandogya Upanishad** affirms this *(VI.8.4)*: "*All beings have their root in the "Sath" (Brahman), that they abide in the "Sath," and they are grounded in the "Sath."*

- "The *Sath* brings forth the universe by its Will (*sankalpa*). According to the Visishtaadvaita theory of cosmic evolution, creation is not the production of something new from what does not exist but on the contrary, it is the unfolding of what already exists in an unmanifest form.

- All beings, sentient and insentient, *cit* and *acit* (in the universe of *prakruti*) exist in Brahman in their subtle form, and Brahman by his *sankalpa*, causes their evolution into the manifested form.

- Brahman is, therefore, the material cause of the universe (*upaadaana kaarana*), and all beings proceed from it… they have their being in Brahman and are sustained by it."

UNQUOTE

All the other *Vishnu Sahasranaama* epithets found in the same **90th shloka** --- viz. *"anuh", "brihat", "krisah",* *"stulah"* and *"mahaan"* – all of them, in fact, variously connote the very same above meanings only.

"apprthk siddhi" and "sarira-sariri-bhaava":

Again, I quote from S.M.S.Chari's book which explains this twin-principle very lucidly:

- "According to Visishtaadvaita epistemology, a substance is inseparable from its attribute. If we take the example of a *blue lotus*, the *blueness* which is the attribute of lotus cannot exist independently except as inherent in the lotus. In the same way, lotus as a substance cannot be conceived devoid of the *blue color*. The two together always coexist (*apprthak-stithi*) and are seen as integrally related (*apprthk prateeti*).

- "*Apprthak-siddhi*" is thus a name given to two relata that are inherently and inseparably related. This is the type of relation that holds good between "*jeeva*," the soul, and the physical body, the '*sarira.*' On this analogy of "*jeeva*" (*sariri*) and the body (*sarira*), the relationship that exists between Brahman and the rest of the universe of *cit* and *acit* is also described in the Visishtaadvaita Vedanta as "*sarira-sariribhaava-sambhandha.*"

- The metaphysical implication of it is that Brahman is always inseparably related to the universe (*prakruti*) of sentient souls and insentient matter. This means that both in the state of creation and the state after the creation of the universe, Brahman is associated with *cit* and *acit*.

- In the state prior to creation, the *cit* and *acit* abide with Brahman in a subtle form and Brahman in that state is associated with *cit* and *acit* in their subtle state (*sookshma-cid-acid-visishta*) …. This is again, *vide* the *Sahasranaama* name of "*anuh*" (839th *naama*).

- In the state after the Creation of the universe, Brahman abides with the manifested *cit* and *acit* in their gross form (*sthoola-cid-acid-visishta*). ... And this too, again, is *vide* the Sahasranaama name of "*sthula*" (842nd *naama*)

- Brahman (thus) is always (*sarvadaa*) associated with *cit* and *acit* ... And as "*jagatkaaranan,*" the primary cause of the universe through pure Will (*ikshana* or *sankalpa*); and as "*visishta-Brahman*" too (i.e., not as pure *un-differentiated* Being), organically related to the universe of *cit* and *acit* by virtue of its being the ground (*aadhaara*) and controller (*Eshaana*), He (as "*purushottama*) is indeed the Ultimate Reality of Visishtaadvaita metaphysics.

****

Student: Sir, I have a fleeting shadow of doubt in my mind while trying to grasp the Visishtaadvaita principles of "*apprthak-siddhi*" and "*sarira-sariri-bhaava*" above.

Unknown Sri Vaishnava: What is it? Go ahead and ask.

Student: In common sensory, worldly experience there is what, in modern psychology, is called "**psychosomatism**." It is a branch of study relating to or concerned with the influence of the mind on the body, and the body on the mind (especially with respect to disease).

For example, it is commonly known that physical ailments or disorders, such as stomach ulcers, are thought to be caused or aggravated by psychological factors such as stress, depressed states of mind, etc. A major cause of diabetes is said to be caused by chronic mental stress.

From such a common experience of *psychosomatism*, we may be led to think that if there is a *Body-Mind* connect, could there also not be a similar conditional connection between *Sarira* and *Sariri* – the *Body* and the *Soul* of a *jeevaatma*?

If there were indeed such kind of a connect, would not "*apprathak-siddhi*" between *Brahman* (the *sariri*) and *Prakruti* (the *sarira*) imply that the imperfections and taint of the "*triguna-s*" of the latter do influence or otherwise affect the "*suddha-sattva*" or blemish-less, auspicious nature and qualities ("*akhila-heya-pratyaneeka kalyaana guna-ganaan*") of the former?

Unknown Sri Vaishnava: To remove such niggling, and tad perverse doubts, the Visishtaadvaitin would refer you to the authority of the **Chandogya Upanishad** *(8-1-5)* **and the Vedanta-sutra** *(III.2.18 and 20):*

"*esha atma apahata paapma vijaro vimrityur visoko vijighatso pipasah: satya kaamah satya sankalpa*"

The Upanishad declares Brahman as "***apahatapaapma,***" i.e., *untouched by imperfection or evil*. This is explained by two analogies of the Sun and Space.

In the first illustration, the sun is seen to be reflected in the multitude of waves of water on earth, but the defects or pollutants found in the water waves do not affect the Sun in any way. The Sun is not actually present in the waves but is only being seen to be resident inside them as so many mirrored reflection --- i.e., "*guna-darpana*" -- and it is just so that the Paramaatman too, with its infinitude of qualities, is resident, or mirrored *or reflected*, in all the entities of *prakruti* and yet is never really part of them. The analogy is intended to convey the fact that movements, colors, currents, spate, etc. found in the waves, do not apply to the Sun.

In the second example, the space (*aakaasa*) when conditioned by several earthen pots of varying sizes becomes manifold; but the differences in the dimension of the receptacles do not apply to Space *per se* nor do they ever become a measure of it in any conceivable sense.

In the same way, Brahman though immanent in all the beings and Matter in the universe remains ever unaffected, untainted, and unconditioned by any of the conditioning qualities of the tri-*guna*-s in which "*prakruti*"is bound.

Thus, it must be understood that although the relationship between "*sariri*" and "*sarira*" is **organic** per the principle of "*apprathak-siddhi*," it is certainly not to be conflated ever with being **psychosomatic** in the modern sense of the term.

Dialogue 8

The Polemics of the *"Nirguna"* Debate

Unknown Sri Vaishnava: You asked the question, *"What is the polemical exchange about between the Advaita and Visishtaadvaita schools of Vedanta on the issue of whether Brahman is without Guna or abounds in glorious, an infinitude of Gunas?"*

So let me try and explain it all to you to the best of my knowledge and ability owed to my guru and other mentors.

****

The polemics between the two schools of Vedanta forms the main subject of *"tarka-vaadaa-*s," the many dialectical disputations in the *"satadushani"* of Vedanta Desika … viz. *Nos. 1, 2, 38, 45, 48, 52, 57, 58, 59, and 66.*

The *"vaadaas"* themselves are too formidable and technically complex for us to discuss in detail. They are meant to be studied in what within Sri Vaishnava theological academies are known to be formal and extensive seminars called *"grantha kaalashepam"* conducted by an *achaarya* for his small band of qualified disciples he himself carefully selects. So, for the extremely limited purpose of our dialogue, I will only summarize the polemics in a very general sort of way in the larger context of the primary question posed right at the outset when you and I began this lengthy conversation viz.:

"If Brahman has no attributes (Nirguna brahman), how is the Advaitin's statement to be reconciled with the "anantha kalyaana guna-s" of Brahman posited by the Visishtaadvaitin?"

The short and simple answer to the above question is, frankly speaking, just this:

- There is no possibility, none whatsoever, of reconciling the Advaitin and Visishtaadvaitin positions about *Nirguna Brahman*.

- The reason is that the two philosophers engage in polemics based on mutually exclusive premises and interpretations of the authority of the *"sruti"* or Upanishad *"vaakya-*s."

The whole of the Visishtaadvaitin's position about this debate is based on the premise of reasonability viz. (1) **"*sruti ekavaakyatvam*"**, whereas the whole of the philosophy of Advaita in fact, is implacably premised on the postulate called (2) **"*brahma ekatvam*"**.

Thus, like the *East is East and West is West*, the two schools likewise, *the twain shall never meet.*

Nonetheless, since you wish to know, in a very general way, about the substance of the polemics between the two Vedanta schools, let us examine the matter in a little more detail.

****

The *"ekavaakyatvam"* premise has already been explained in an earlier dialogue (*Dialogue 5*) above, but it is exactly what the *"satadushani"* also bases all its *"vaada-s"* upon. Vedanta Desikan admits that there are *"sruti"* texts which declare Brahman to be devoid of qualities e.g.

- *"nishkalam nishkriyam shaantam niravadyam niranjanam..."* (**Svetasvataara Upanishad VI.19**)

- *"yattad-adreseyam agraahyam agotram avarnam achaakshuhu ashrotram tadapaanipaadam..."*
  (**Mundakopanishad I.1.6**)

- *"apahatapaapmaa vijarah...."* (**Chandogya Upanishad 8.1.7**)

- *"asthoolam ananu...."* (**Brhadaaranyaka Upanishad 5.8.8**)

There are also *"sruti vaakyas"* that openly declare Brahman to be qualified by numerous attributes:

- *"yas sarvagnyaanah sarvavith satyakaamas-sathya-sankalpah..."* (**Mundakopanishad 2.2.7**)
  - Chandogya **Upanishad – 8.1.5**
  - Svetasvataara **Upanishad – 6.8**
  - Taittiriya **Upanishad – I.1.2**

****

Sri Ramanuja in his **Vedaartha-Sangraha** has explained how in the various *"srutis,"* the nature of Brahman is conceived and spoken of in *six diverse ways*! And at times when read cursorily, they could be easily misunderstood and misinterpreted as being mutually contradictory.

Ramanuja classifies the relevant *"sruti"* passages into the following categories:

A. "There is one group of texts which describes Brahman as **attribute-less** and as being of the nature of pure Knowledge. (Passage 109)

B. There is another type of text which **denies plurality** to Brahman. (Passage 110)

C. There is another class of "srutis" which denies Brahman of everything that may be thought to be evil or unvirtuous in the world. It also predicates Brahman with **infinite and surpassingly auspicious attributes**, of which omniscience and omnipotence are only a few, and which Brahman alone is the author of all differentiations of the universe in terms of names, forms, and attributes... and is verily the support of all. (Passage 111)

D. There is again, another variety of srutis that describe the universe being created by Brahman in all its multiplicities and, at the same time, also affirm its **essential One-ness**. (Passage 112)

E. Then there are some texts which maintain that Brahman is **distinct from all that exists**, and yet that which is existent is **subordinate** to Him, while he is their supreme ruler. And that all entities -- sentient, insentient, material, and non-material -- all are subsidiary to him, while he is their master. (Passage 113)

F. Lastly, there are sruti texts which declare Brahman to be the self of all entities and that all entities in the universe **constitute merely his body.** (Passage 114)

****

At this point in the dialogue, the student interjected and asked the Unknown Sri Vaishnava a pointed question.

Student: Sir, I have a doubt.

Unknown Sri Vaishnava: Go ahead, ask.

Student: It is about what has been said in **C. above**.

Unknown Sri Vaishnava: What about it? It is exactly what Ramanujacharya has written in his "*Vedaartha Sangraha*" in **Passage 111** as quoted.

Student: Sir, can you please explain a little more about what exactly the "*sruti*" means which Ramanuja alludes to? I.e. that it "*predicates Brahman with infinite and surpassingly auspicious attributes, of which omniscience and omnipotence are only a few…*"?

Unknown Sri Vaishnava: I am so happy you have paused me here to ask this question! It is very pertinent! And it gives me the perfectly timed opportunity to explain to you another uniquely Visishtaadvaitic interpretation of the "*sruti vaakya*" pertaining to the ontological nature of Brahman through a doctrine called "**ubhayalingatva sutra**" found in the **Vedanta-Sutra** (vide: **III. 2.11** – "*na sthaanato'pi parasyobhayalingam sarvatra hi….*").

This *sutra* has been interpreted extensively by Ramanujacharya in his **Sri Bhaashya**. S.M.S.Chari's in his book "*Sri Vaishnavism*" summarizes it as follows:

QUOTE

The sruti and smriti texts describe the nature of Brahman to be free from any kind of imperfection (*samasta-heya-pratyaaneeka*). Brihadaaranyaka Upanishad says, "*Brahman is neither gross not minute, neither short nor long.*" The Mundaka Upanishad describes the imperishable higher Reality as "unperceivable, ungraspable, without family lineage (*agotram*), without caste, without sight or hearing, without hands or feet, etc." The Chaandogya Upanishad states that Brahman is "free from sin, free from old age, free from death, free from sorrow, free from hunger, free from thirst." The *Vishnu Purana* explicitly mentions that the nature of Vishnu is free from all imperfections. Now taking into consideration these negative descriptions of Brahman, Ramanuja takes the view that **defectless-ness** or "*heya-pratyaneekatva*" itself constitutes an essential attribute of Brahman because it serves to distinguish Brahman from the universe comprising the souls and non-sentient matter. Accordingly, Brahman thus has a two-fold aspect in its essential nature --- '*ubhayalingam*,' as declared in the Vedanta Sutra – that it is ***absolutely free from defects***, and it is also ***endowed with innumerable auspicious attributes***."

"The *Paancharaatra Agamas* have mentioned six attributes (by way of just a small example of those innumerable auspicious qualities) as particularly important. These are: "**gnyaana**" (omniscience), "**bala**" (omnipotence), "**aiswarya**" (Omni-resourceful), "**veerya**" (Omni-valorous), **tejas** (Omni-splendorous) and **shakti** (Omni-powerful) …. According to the *Paancharaatra* treatises, the possession of these six qualities makes the Supreme Being perfect – **a Paragon** -- in all respects."

UNQUOTE

Unknown Sri Vaishnava: Let us continue. Ramanuja then proceeds to emphatically affirm the "*meemaamsa*" rule of interpreting '*sruti vaakya*" strictly according to the holistic doctrine of "*ekavaakyatvam*" in the following words in **Passage 114**:

QUOTE:

"The interpretation of the several types of texts must be such that they are not made to contradict one another themselves both in content and intent; and that not a single text should be so interpreted as to be divested of its primary and fundamental significance".

UNQUOTE

The most powerful argument Ramanuja makes is the one found in a passage where he exhibits extraordinary conviction while lucidly expounding and defending the metaphysics of Visishtaadvaita Vedanta against the postulate of Advaitic *"nirgunatvam"* (**Passage 117** of the *Vedaartha Sangraham*). The passage is a masterpiece indeed:

QUOTE:

- "It may be asked (of me), "What is your final position? Do you uphold the *Unity* or the *Plurality*, or *both Unity and Plurality* of Brahman? Which of these three forms does the substance of your Vedanta interpretation stand on?

- "And I reply that I *uphold all the three* as they are *all affirmed in the Veda.*

- "I uphold *Unity* because Brahman alone exists, with everything else in the universe of *"prakruti"* being only its various modes.

- "I uphold *both Unity and Plurality* since the One Brahman itself has all the spiritual and physical substances as its mere modes and, hence, thereby itself exists as qualified by plurality.

- "I uphold *plurality* in so far as the three categories of existence viz. sentient beings and non-sentient matter along with the supreme Lord (*"chith"*, *"a-chith"* and *"Isvara"*), all exist and are mutually distinct from each other in their substantive nature and attributes, yet with no mutual transposition of their characteristics."

UNQUOTE

****

The Unknown Sri Vaishnava: Now, in the **Satadushani** too, Vedanta Desika states that *saguna srutis* are as valid as the *nirguna srutis* in as much as both refer to the same Reality. Both texts must be interpreted in such a way that the apparent conflict does not arise at all --- thus abiding with the axiom of "*ekavaakyatvam.*"

But then the Advaitin does not give up. He contends that it is the *nirguna* set of texts that have superior validity and it is the *saguna* texts which must be held to be non-authoritative. Both texts cannot be maintained as equally valid since what they signify is mutually exclusive and hence one of them, the *saguna sruti vaakyas* are the ones that must be negated and stand as invalid.

Now, when asked why, the Advaitin replies that it is because Adi Sankara himself in his commentary on the Vedanta-Sutra has held it to be so. According to Sankara, there is only *Nirguna Brahman*. There is no *Saguna Brahman*.

Adi Sankara Bhagavathpaada

QUOTE

- *"Brahman is only formless to be sure, for that is the dominant note (of the Upanishadic teaching).* Why?

- "*For that is the dominant teaching*", in as much as it has been established under the aphorism, "*But that Brahman is known from the Upanishads, because of their being connected with Brahman as their main import*" *(I.i.4)*; that the texts like the following have for their main purport the transcendental Brahman which is the Self, and not any subject matter: *"It is neither gross, nor minute, neither short nor long"* **(Br. III.viii.8),** "Soundless, touchless, colorless, undiminishing" **(Katha I.iii.15)** .... And so on.

- "Hence in sentences of this kind, the formless Brahman alone, just as it is spoken by the texts themselves, has to be accepted. But the other texts, speaking of Brahman with form, have the injunctions about *meditations* as their main objectives. So long as they do not lead to a contradiction, their apparent meanings should be accepted. But when they involve a contradiction, *the principle to be followed for deciding one or the other is that those that have the formless Brahman as their main* purport are **more authoritative than the others** which have not that as their main purport. It is according to this that one is driven to the conclusion that Brahman is formless and not its opposite, though texts having both the purports are in evidence.

"Brahma Sutra Bhaashya of Sri Sankaracharya" ... III.ii.14 translated by **Swami Gambhirananda**)

****

Student: Sir, what exactly is the ***principle*** that you say is involved when Adi Sankara proclaims that those <u>sruti</u> <u>vaakyas</u> that have the formless Brahman as their main purport are more authoritative than the others?

Unknown Sri Vaishnava: The Advaitin's principles are based on this:

- "Sruti vaakya-*s*" *which deny all qualities to Brahman appear* later *in the order of texts than the texts which refer to Brahman as qualified. Denial presupposes that which is to be denied.* Negation follows Affirmation *and **what comes later is of greater force** and occupies the position of the "sublater" sublating the earlier. This conclusion is according to the rule of logic and grammar laid down in a scriptural rule of hermeneutics called "***apaccheda-nyaaya***."*

- *The Visishtaadvaitin argues that the "appaccheda-nyaaya" does not apply at all in the case here since it holds water only where two texts that are not regularly opposed to each other follow as the earlier and later. In other words, what occurs later cannot arise except as contradicting what occurs earlier.*

- *For example, in the two statements "**This is silver**" and "**This is not silver**," the latter text in denying the earlier, would be more valid since the later cognition cannot arise except as sublating the earlier and as such what gets sublated cannot be regarded in any case as valid.*

- *However, where there is regular opposition between the two texts coming as earlier and later, it is the earlier text that is to be held predominant. This is as per the principle of* "**upakramaadhi-karana-nyaaya**."

- *Now, in the present case, saguna and nirguna texts are two mutually and regularly opposed to each other by their very nature and significance. So, the question of the later being stronger than the earlier does not arise at all.*

- *The **Satadushani** proceeds to tell the Advaitin that in deciding the merits of the rules of interpretation in the present case, it is really neither "**appaccheda**" nor "**upakramaadhi**" "**nyaaya**" rules that are apt. It is another principle known as "**utsargaa-pavaada-nyaaya**" that offers a better solution to the problem.*

- *According to this principle, the negative text will have to be interpreted in accordance with the affirmative text. If some "sruti" texts affirm that Brahman possesses attributes while others deny the same, the latter should be understood to mean the denial of attributes other than those mentioned or signified by the former.*

- *The implication of the "nirguna" texts, therefore, is that Brahman is **devoid of inauspicious or imperfect qualities** .... And it is not that Brahman is devoid of **all qualities**. That way the validity of both the "sruti vaakyaas" is maintained.*

- *If on the contrary, the principle of the later sublating the earlier is adopted, it will simply not be possible to maintain the validity of both "sruti" texts in accordance with the overarching axiom of Vedantic hermeneutics, "**ekavaakyatvam**."*

Unknown Sri Vaishnava: Is your doubt now cleared?

Student: Yes, sir. Thank you.

Unknown Sri Vaishnava: All right then, let me proceed.

****

Next, during the long-drawn, *100-"vaadaa"-debate* between the Advaitin and Visishtaadvaitin, arises the cardinal question of **"*brahma ekatvam*"** --- or what the former terms it as "*brahma adviteeyam*" echoing the "*sruti vaakya*": **"*ekam-eva adviteeyam*"** --- "*Brahman is One without a second*".

- According to Advaita philosophy that statement incontrovertibly implies that Brahman is indeed "*nirguna*" and "*nirvisesha*" since if that One Reality of Brahman alone exists (*sath*) and everything else is only an illusion of reality (*asath* conjured by *maaya*), there can never be anything existent other than the One itself to qualify or characterize it.

The Visishtaadvaitin rejects such Advaitic interpretation of *"adviteeyam"* as fallacious and illogical.

The *Satadushani* (*vaada* 59) cites the staunch support for such rejection found in the famous statement of the grand-guru of Ramanujacharya, **Sri Yaamunaachaarya** (aka *Alavandaar* – early 10th century CE), who in his seminal work on Vaishnava metaphysics, "**Siddhitraya**" wrote:

"yathaa cholanrpah samraat adviteeyotra bhutale.

Iti tattulya nrpati nivaarana param vachah.

na tu tad-bhrtya-tatputra kalatraadi nishedhakam."

"The paramount ruler of the Chola kingdom now reigning is without a second in this world;" this statement is only intended to deny the existence of a ruler equal to him; it does not deny the existence of his servants, sons, consorts, armies, palaces and so on…"

Yamunancharya went on then to explain it all himself:

QUOTE:

"Adviteeya" **is one who neither has, nor had, nor will have an equal or superior capable of being counted as a second."** In other words, what the *sruti* intends to convey is that no second similar, equal, or superior entity to Brahman exists (*"sadrsha dviteeya nisheda param"*). But, in the statement, *"There is but a single Sun in the sky and not two,"* there the presence of a single sun and no more is not being contradicted at all, but then does it also mean that the sunrays, the heat, the dazzling light, the warmth, etc. too must all be denied?! That would be illogical.

Similarly, when the *sruti* declares Brahman to be *"adviteeya," without a second*, the existence of His attributes or qualities are not denied. All it means is that there is nothing in the universe that can be similar or equated with Brahman." **UNQUOTE**

Yet another intensely debated question between the Advaitin and Visishtaadvaitin as described in Vedanta Desika's *"satadushani vaadaa-s"* is the one recorded in **Vaada No.38** under the heading *"akhandaartham"* where the two schools battle it out over a certain rule of interpretation known as ***"saamaanaadhi-karanya"***.

It is an interesting and illuminative debate shedding great light on the meaning of the famous and oft-quoted Upanishad *vaakya* found in the *"Anandavalli"* passage in the **Taittiriya Upanishad.** It is the tersest and yet most revealing Vedantic definition of Brahman found in all the extant 108 Upanishads of India.

ब्रह्मविदाप्नोति परम् । तदेषाऽभ्युक्ता । सत्यं ज्ञानमनन्तं ब्रह्म।

One who knows Brahman, reaches the highest. **Satya** *(reality, truth) is Brahman,* **Jnana** *(knowledge) is Brahman,* **Ananta** *(infinite) is Brahman.*

— *Taittiriya Upanishad, 2.1.1*

- *Sathyam* means, according to Ramanuja, the *non-conditioned existence* of Brahman. It is an eternal, self-existent, and self-contained ontological entity without being subjected to any kind of change or modification (*vikaara*). This distinguishes Brahman from the rest of the universe of beings – *cit* and *acit* – which undergo all manner of *"vikaara,"* and continuous modifications caused through both the cycle of birth, death, and rebirth as well through the operation of the *triguna-s*.

- *Gnyaana*, according to Ramanuja, means eternal and fulsome Knowledge or *"sarvagnyata"* (*omniscience*) which is *never subject to either contraction or expansion* utterly unlike the knowledge of finite, sentient beings, or human souls in the universe. The term "*sarvagnyata*" has an extremely specific meaning in Visishtaadvaita philosophy derived from the Mundaka Upanishad which says that Brahman knows everything since it has the capacity to comprehend everything in the universe as it is always, by intuition and without the aid of the sense organs (as all sentient and intelligent beings in the universe otherwise must depend upon).

- Brahman is also **Anantham** or infinite because it is omnipresent, it always exists, is never conditioned by time or space or by any other entity, and pervades all other entities in the universe.

****

The main issue with the above Upanishad "*vaakya*" that has been a perennial cause of disagreement between Advaitin and Visishtaadvaitin is that in defining Brahman as "*Truth, Knowledge,* and *Infinitude*," the former says it denotes the "*svarupa*" or the **nature** of Brahman only while the latter says it denotes the **nature** of Brahman **with reference to the characteristics/attributes** or "*guna*" of Brahman.

- According to Visishtaadvaita, Brahman is both "*gnyaana-svarupa*" and "*gnyaana-gunaka*" (*vide* "**sruta-prakaasika**" **I.1.1**). Not only the *svarupa* (nature) of Brahman but also its attributes are *infinite* (*anantham*) in the sense that they are countless and unsurpassable in excellence and perfection. The three named characteristics are thus unique to Brahman, and they reveal its true nature (*svarupa-niroopaka-dharma*), no doubt, but then if the Visishtaadvaitin were asked what the nature of Brahman is, his categorical answer would be that **Brahman is that which is characterized by "*satyatva, gnyaanatva,* and *anantatva.*"**

- Such an interpretation of the Upanishad "*vaakya*" as given above by the Visishtaadvaitin is not, however, acceptable to the Advaitin for whom these 3 terms denote only the mere "*svarupa*" or *nature* of Brahman and *in no way do they characterize it.*

- According to him, the Upanishad "*vaakya*" means only that Brahman **is** "*sathyam, gnyaanam* and *anantham*" *per se* and it does not mean that it is ***possessed***, *ipso facto,* of these three *characteristics*. Why? Because, the Advaitin firmly avers, of a certain abstruse rule in Vedantic hermeneutics called **"*saamaanyaadi-karanya*"** by which Advaita philosophy solemnly and rigidly swears.

****

What is this *"saamaanyaadi-karanya"*? It is a rule of grammar … or "*vyaakarana*", which relates to how a statement is made and what it truly signifies.

In the statement, for example, "*He is Devadutta*," the two terms "*he*" and "*devadutta*" both stand in "*apposition*" to each other, they are "*impartite*" and they are "*non-relational*."

"Apposition" means a grammatical construction of a sentence in which two usually adjacent nouns having the same referent, stand in the same syntactical relation to the rest of a sentence.

"Impartite" means not partible: not subject to partition.

"Non-relational" means the two terms are not having any relation to each other as both in significance are the same.

"*He is Devadatta*" thus conveys the idea of one entity only since all the constituent terms of the sentence denote the same thing.

Therefore, Advaitin argues, the Upanishad *vaakya* should be equally understood to mean that Brahman is verily "*satyam,*" "*gnyaanam,*" "*anantham*" itself and should not be construed as meaning that Brahman is possessed of the three attributes. Brahman is thus one homogenous entity being devoid of all differentiation (*nirguna/nirvisesha*).

****

The Visishtaadvaitin however does not agree.

He says that not only is the Advaitin's definition and understanding of the rule of "*saamaanyaadi-karanya*" fallacious but the way he even exemplifies and applies it is misleading.

In the "*satadushani*," there are many *vaada*-s that criticize elaborately the Advaitin's position. Without going into their details, what is possible to observe as being the nub of the Visishtaadvaitin counter is this:

- Terms in a sentence where they stand in "*apposition,*" do not convey an "*impartite*" and "*non-relational* sense." Though the terms in the statement have different connotations, they can yet denote the same thing.

- For example, in the sentence "This is *blue lotus* ("*nilotpalam*")," the term "*blue*" has a different connotation from that of the term "*lotus*." The connotation of "*blue*" is that quality of "*blue-ness*" while that of "*lotus*" is "*lotus-ness*" and yet the two terms (in apposition) refer to one object viz.; the **Lotus**.

- It is such terms that are said to be "*saamaanyaadi-karanya.*"

- Therefore, contrary to what is understood by the Advaitin, if one applies the "*saamaanyaadi-karanya*" rule to the Upanishad *vaakya* of सत्यं ज्ञानमनन्तं ब्रह्म, one will have to accept that it denotes one entity, being the *svarupa* (nature) of Brahman, as qualified by its characteristics (*guna*) connoted by the other three terms in the sentence viz. *Truth, Knowledge, and Infinitude*. Such indeed is the true meaning of "*saamaanyaadi-karanya*" where, in a sentence, the terms having different connotations, denote one thing.

****

Unknown Sri Vaishnava: And that, my dear young man, in summary and substance, is finally the Advaita-Visishtaadvaita polemical exchange on the metaphysical issue of **Nirguna Brahman**. It is indeed the foundational and most significant philosophical rift -- or call it fault-line, if you like -- between the two Vedanta schools or "*darsana*-s". Perhaps because of its definitive nature, it is a dispute which will never be reconciled and put to rest.

Student: I thank you, Sir, for explaining to me the concept of *Nirguna Brahman* in Vedanta philosophy, so clearly and patiently. Our conversation has indeed been most illuminating and fascinating.

****

Epilogue

The Unknown Sri Vaishnava: The purpose and motives in my recording of the series of long dialogues with a student-friend of mine on the topic of the Visishtaadvaita view on **Nirguna Brahman** are as follows:

As I reach an age in life today when true concerns of *"atma vichaara"* (personal philosophical inquiry) begin to weigh heavily upon my mind a lot more than they used to hitherto, and then again, as the sense of my own individual mortality grows stronger by the day and begins to loom much larger than ever before, the question of *"nirgunatvam"* no longer is mere philosophical will o' the-wisp. It is now an idea whose time has come to confront squarely in the face. It assumes relevance and urgency to me as would a cardinal article of faith matter to a soul trying to grasp at the truth. More specifically, it raises in my mind quite a few searing questions such as the following:

- *When I die, what will happen to the senses with the aid of which alone, all my life, I have apprehended and experienced all reality?*

- *If Brahman alone is real and all else illusion, all my life then, have I been experiencing only "mithyaa" or hallucinations all along with my senses and mind? Is human life then nothing but what the Persian poet, Omar Khayyam dolefully described it to be:*

There was a Door to which I found no key.
There was a Veil through which I might not see.
Some talk there was awhile of Thee and Me…
Then there was no more of Thee and Me.

- *After my senses and my mind cease to exist, what will remain? Nothingness? And what is the nature of that Nothing-ness which alone according to the Advaitin is real? Is it just subjective "Consciousness" with no object at all? A nameless, un-differentiated, non-relational, attribute-less entity called noumenal "gnyaana"?*

- *The Taittireeya Upanishad says that I came from Brahman, that my life here was always rooted in Brahman, and that when I depart from here, I shall enter again into Brahman… **"yato vaa imaani jaayante; yena jaataani jeevanti; yat prayantyabhishamti santi….**" And then the Upanishad also urges me **"tath vijignyaasasya…"** It urges me to exert effort in knowing that very Brahman.*

- *Now, I ask myself, if the ultimate reality of Advaitic Brahman is really nothing else but a noumena of undifferentiated, quality-less, **non-descript**, impersonal Consciousness, what purpose is really served by my singing stotra-s, praises, hymns, and hallelujahs to its glories? Of what use is **Bhakti** that even Advaitin theology extols? What use is my singing the glories (i.e., "upaasana" or worshipful meditation) of a Reality that possesses no glorifiable attributes at all?*

It is with such questions playing upon my mind --- "*atma vichaara*" --- I began searching for answers in that most illuminating work of Visishtaadvaita philosophy our "*paramaachaarya,*" Sri Vedanta Desikan wrote: the **Satadushani.**

Studying this work has provided me with clarity and illumination on the many troubling doubts on "*nirgunatvam*" often surfacing in my mind. I have found in it, at last, a cogent and convincing explication of why "*Brahman*" of the Upanishads and the Vedanta-sutra cannot be "*nirguna*" or "*nirvisesha*" … That Brahman must truly be what Sri Ramanujacharya himself celebrated *in*, and *as*, his very own personal experience. He shared it with all humankind too in one memorable passage in his "***saranaagathi gadyam***," a mystical outpouring in Sanskrit of extraordinary spiritual insight, a spontaneous, and effusive outpouring, and an epiphany that took hold of him and revealed itself in the idol of Sri Ranganatha as it came around the streets of the temple of **Sri Rangam**:

"**svAbhAvika anavadhikAtiSaya jn~Ana bala aiSvarya vIrya Sakti teja: sauSIlya**

vAtsalya mArdava Arjava sauhArda sAmya kAruNya mAdhurya gAmbhIrya

audArya cAturya sthairya dhairya Saurya parAkrama satyakAma satyasankalpa

krtitva krtajn~atAdyasamkhyeya kalyANa guNagaNaugha mahArNava!"

Thou art the Ocean unto which flow rivers of limitless excellent virtues, all

That are natural to Thee; effective for protection of your devotees, perfect virtues such as Omniscience, Omnipotence, untiring virility, Power to act

At Will, yet kindly disposed towards all thy creation, your compassion akin to that of a cow's love and care for its calf.

****

Subhamastu!

****

Acknowledgments

Many people extended their kindness to me in conceiving, writing, finessing, and finally publishing this book. Without their immensely valuable contribution this book would never have been possible to publish and I must express my deep gratitude to them.

His Holiness Srimad Azhagiyasingar, the present and 46th Pontiff of Sri Ahobla Mutt, who blessed this book with his Grace in the form of a benedictory *"Sri Mukham"* a facsimile of which appears as the first page in this book.

Sri.Sadagopan Iyengar, Editor of the *"Sri Nrisimha Priya"* (the official English language magazine of the Sri Ahobila Mutt) who readily agreed to pen a Preface for this book. It is both truly eloquent and erudite and it serves as an excellent curtain-raiser to this book.

Sri. U.Ve. Dr. S. Padmanabhachar, the respected, presently serving *"Sri Kaaryam"* of the Ahobila Mutt, who after perusing through the first manuscript of this book was so generous and kind to offer very many excellent suggestions for the improvement and embellishment of both its content and substance.

Sri. Srinivasa Parthasarathy, a retired banker, a doyen, and deep scholar of Hindu scripture and literature who now lives in Pondicherry. It was he who triggered an expansive series of online private conversations on the subject of *"nirguna brahman"* leading eventually to the publication of this book.

Sri.K.Vaidyanath (former Finance Director, ITC Ltd.), a very dear friend, long-term boss, colleague, and fellow student in Vedantic studies, who was the first one to read the manuscript, critique it, and suggested it to be completely re-written in the form of an *Upanishadic Dialogue* rather than as a series of dense essays as I had originally written it.

My wife, **Divya Sudarshan,** and children, son **Shreyas** and daughter, **Harini**, who kept reassuring me that a book of this sort would be worth publishing despite the skepticism and misgivings I had had about the whole idea. They insisted that a book such as this would certainly appeal to many youngsters like themselves since it would help them appreciate basic tenets of Sri Ramanujacharya's Visishtaadvaitic philosophy and its fine, subtle and unique metaphysics found in texts such as the ***Satadushani*** and the ***Bhagavath-Guna-Darpana***, scarcely read at all by today's youth.

****

Bibliography

1. **Bhagavath Guna Darpana** by Parashara Bhatta
2. S.M. Srinivasa Chari – *"Visishtaadavaita and Advaita"*
3. S.M. Srinivasachari – *"Vaishnavism- Its Philosophy, Theology and Religious Discipline"*
4. Prof. K.V. Rangaswami Ayyangar – *"Rajadharma"*
5. Vedanta Desika – *"Satadushani"*
6. *Vishnu Sahasranaama: Bhagavath Guna Darpana* – commentary by Parashara Bhatta (translation in English by Prof. A. Srinivasa Raghavan) – published by **Sri Visishtaadvaita Pracharini Sabha, Madras, 1983)**
7. Sri Ramanujacharya's *"Vedaartha Sangraha"* – translated in English by S.S. Raghavachar – published by **Advaita Ashram, Kolkata, 2002**
8. Dr. S. Radhakrishnan – *"History of Indian Philosophy"*
9. *"Saundaryalahari"* – An Exposition by Pujyasri Chandrasekharendra Sarasvati Swami, 68th Sankaracharya of Kanchi Kamakoti Pitha – **Bharati Vidya Bhavan publication (2012)**
10. *"What the Buddha Taught"* - Walpola Rahula : (2006)- **Buddhist Cultural Centre, Nedimala, Dehiwala, Sri Lanka**

About the Author:

M. K. Sudarshan is a graduate of the Madras University from Loyola College, Chennai, and a qualified Chartered Accountant. After a 35+years long and successful international career in corporate finance, he now lives with his wife in Chennai, pursuing wider interests in Indian philosophy, world history and comparative religious literature, studies, and writing. His related interests are classical South Indian music, the history of Hindu temples in India and travelling worldwide.

Sudarshan traces his ancestral roots in his native town in Tirupati to the forebears on the paternal side of his family through his grandmother to the *"Thozhappachariars"* of **Tirumala-Tirupati** who were the descendants of the maternal uncle of Sri Ramanujachaarya, *Sri Tirumalai Nambi* (11th century CE) and to the *"Madabhooshi-vamsha"* through his paternal grandfather who was a leading lawyer in Tirupati. Sudarshan is the son of the renowned Carnatic Musician Sangita Kalanidhi, (late) **Smt. Mani Krishnaswami**, who was the Asthaana Vidwan of the Tirumala Temple and the Ahobila Math.

Other published book of the author on Sri Vaishnavism: "*Unusual Essays of an Unknown Sri Vaishnava*" (2021 – **Mainspring Books, LA, USA**)

REVIEWS of *"The Unusual Essays Of An Unknown Sri Vaishnava"*

(First Edition: 2016)

"A book of personal essays on subjects related to a particular Hindu sect …. Many touch on thinkers from the Western canon, as well. William Blake, William Shakespeare, and William Wordsworth all receive mentions, and it's in this blending of influences that the book achieves its unique, inviting perspective …. Enlightening dive into *Sri Vaishnavism*."

KIRKUS INDIE REVIEW (April 2018) Https://Www.Kirkusreviews.Com/Book-Reviews/Mk-Sudarshan/Unusual-Essays-Unknown-Sri-Vaishnava/

****

"……this book is certainly an engrossing read with the most complex of philosophies, practices, culture and other aspects of a global citizen's daily life explained in an engaging yet easily comprehensible style of the author."

Dr M. Varadarajan

"*The Hindu*" (August 2017)

(India's National Newspaper Since 1878)

Http://Www.Thehindu.Com/Books/Books-Reviews/Rituals-Associated-With-Vaishnavism/Article19464016.Ece

****

"(This book) is a journey of discovery.... The search (for the author) that began two decades ago, continues...."

--- News Today, *Chennai*—May, 2017.

****

"The book .... Has the unique distinction of receiving the blessings and appreciation of the presiding Pontiffs of all 3 principal and extant vedantic schools in India --- *Visishtadaita, Advaita and Dvaita*: Sri Ahobila Mutt, Sri Sankaraacharya Mutt, Sringeri and Udupi Sri Pejaawar Mutt"

"Mylapore Talk", Chennai, Dec 2017

****

"The author brings to bear a refreshingly new focus on various traditional concepts and scriptures while taking care to toe the traditional (Sri Vaishnava) line mostly, ... With an impeccable language and excellent narrative style.... this book impresses one with its nice turn of phrases, the facile rendering of even difficult ideas in comprehensible terms .... This book would form a welcome addition to anyone's library ... especially useful to expatriate youth of today --- it would help them find their traditional spiritual moorings despite being cast adrift in the ocean of international commerce with no polestar to guide them".

--- **Sadagopan Iyengar,** Editor, "*Nrsimha Priya*": (Official English Journal of Sri Ahobila Mutt, India - Nov 2016)

****

"This book contains a wealth of information in simple language and can fulfill the needs of those who have not been formally tutored in the tenets of *Sri Vaishnavism*... all the fundamentals are illustrated with examples (taken) from the context of the modern world for immediate understanding and association... This volume deserves to be in the collection of those value the hoary heritage and culture of Bharathavarsha...

Dr. Chithra Madhavan

(*TATTVALOKA* (August 2018)

Official magazine of the **Sri Sankaraacharya Mutt** of SRINGERI

****

"This book contains ... in every chapter an abundant wealth of information that is hard to find elsewhere all at one place. The content has rich and resonant quality with its primary focus on "*Bhagavath Ramanuja Darsanam*".... There is a great need today for the kind of simple explanations that Sudarshan is able to offer readers, especially the youthful ones in our families who are so much exposed to the pulls and fleeting attractions of the modern secular world that they find they have little patience for the elaborate profundities of traditional literature. Sudarshan' s essays towards that purpose do succeed in providing help to anyone genuinely seeking to grasp Bhagavath Ramanuja's *sampradaaya* in simple terms in the English language... This is a well compiled book of essays ... and should in my opinion adorn the library of every devout family for in-depth reading at leisure."

Dr. Varadachari Sadagopan

www.sadagopan.org

(Foreword to the First Edition (2016))

****

"This is an absolutely brilliant book… To hold the attention of readers through 700+ pages on a subject as vast and weighty as the author deals with, is impossible… Sudarshan has made the impossible, possible… A gifted writer whose prose is poetic…"

K. Vaidyanath (Ex. Finance Director, ITC Ltd. India)

****

"This book reflects the author's *triump*… not his "*struggle*" … in life in being able to reflect deeply upon, understand Sri Vaishnava philosophy and faith… His ability to connect dots is amazing…"

Shekhar K. Swamy (Managing Director, M/s. RK Swamy BBDO)

A FEW READERS' COMMENTS:

"The whole set of essays beautifully integrates the author's own religious background with the world around him. The easy way in which the Author engulfs all that he sees around him and all the world religions, places, and people is enjoyable. Of course, the array of topics covers a wide range of in-depth themes of the Hindu and the Vaishnavite faiths, without imposing the same on you." (V.Krishnan **Krishnan Venkatachalam** <krish1951@gmail.com>)

"EXCELLENT work. (The author's) command over the subject as well as the languages (English, Sanskrit, and Tamil) is superb. (He has) …written it in such a language that is easily accessible to even a novice like me. The scholarly treatment of the subjects/topics makes it a treat for researchers and laymen alike - A must-read for Advaitins, Vishishtadvaitins, and Dvaitins and all those who are interested in the subject of Vedanta. It is said that – "*Dharmo rakshati rakshitah*" -- By this exquisite work (he is) protecting dharma which in turn will not only protect him but also those who will read this book." (Dr. L.R.Chary <lrchary@gmail.com>)

"It is an exceptional high-octane intellectual journey. Raises several vital philosophical and religious issues with aplomb and venturesome-ness. There is a common thread of viewing our heritage with a discernment that is off-beat. I have just savored a couple of chapters. Shall take time to get engrossed and enjoy this rare treat." (S. Parthasarathy velamur33@gmail.com)

INDEX

aachaara, 46
aahAra-niyamam, 13
aakaasa, 36, 42, 79
acit, 16, 71, 76, 77, 78, 93
adhyaayaa, 42
Advaita, 14, 1, 2, 3, 4, 7, 8, 16, 31, 40, 41, 45, 47, 48, 49, 51, 52, 53, 54, 55, 56, 58, 61, 63, 64, 65, 66, 67, 69, 70, 71, 81, 82, 91, 95, 97, 104, 108
agni, 36
Ahankaaram, 36
akhandaartham, 93
anantha kalyaana guna, 1, 81
anatta, 57
anumaanam, 26
apaccheda-nyaaya, 90
apahatapaapma, 79
Appayya, 5
apprthak-siddhi, 72, 78
Arjuna, 10, 11, 12, 13, 14
arul mozhi, 35
Atma, 45, 50, 54, 56
avidya, 47, 50, 51
Baadaraayana, 14
baddha jeevaatmaa, 36
Bhagavaan, 17, 37
bhagavath guna darpana, 7, 18
Bhagavath-Gita, 9, 14, 16, 22, 62
bhagavath-guna, 19, 20, 22, 24, 29, 33, 34, 35, 70, 71

Bhaja Govindam, 62
bhakti, 14, 39, 66
Bodhaayana, 42
brahma ekatvam, 82, 91
Brahma Sutras, 10, 1, 26
Brahman, 7, 10, 12, 14, 1, 2, 4, 5, 6, 7, 8, 13, 14, 15, 16, 17, 18, 19, 20, 21, 22, 23, 24, 28, 29, 30, 31, 32, 33, 34, 38, 39, 40, 41, 42, 43, 44, 45, 46, 47, 48, 49, 50, 54, 55, 56, 57, 59, 61, 62, 63, 64, 65, 66, 67, 68, 69, 70, 71, 72, 73, 74, 75, 76, 77, 78, 79, 81, 82, 83, 84, 85, 87, 88, 89, 91, 92, 93, 94, 95, 96, 97, 98, 99, 100
Buddhi, 14
Chandogya, 7, 73, 76, 79, 82, 83
Chandogya Upanishad, 73, 76, 79, 82, 83
Chandrasekharendra Saraswathi, 47
cit, 16, 71, 76, 77, 78, 93
Conditioned Genesis, 57, 58, 59, 60, 61
Crypto-Buddhism, 51, 53, 54
dAna, 13
darsana, 5, 42, 63, 70, 97
Dikshita, 5
Dr. S. Radhakrishnan, 52, 104

dukka, 61
Ekavaakyatvam, 45, 46
Gita, 9, 10, 12, 13, 14, 15, 16, 17, 39
GnyAna, 14
guNa, 2, 37
heya-pratyaneekatvam, 22, 40
jagatkaaranatvam, 42, 43, 56, 59, 65, 72, 73, 75
jala, 36
jeevaatma, 8, 56, 78
K.V.Rangaswami Ayyangar, 46
kaala, 37
kalyaana guna, 61, 79
Karma, 50
Kurukshetra, 13, 32, 39
Lakshmi-Narasimha Karaavalamba stotram, 62
Lalita Sahasranaamam, 62
maanaseeka-guru, 3, 4
maaya, 24, 47, 48, 49, 50, 52, 53, 59, 62, 71, 74, 91
maaya shakthi, 59
maayaavada, 51
Mahabharatha, 14, 16
Mahat, 36
mana-prasAdah, 13
Manas, 14
Manthraraaja-pada Stotram, 62
meemaamsa, 3, 5, 46, 52, 86
mithya, 24, 49
moola-prakruthi, 36, 38
mukthi, 37
Mundaka, 7, 51, 85, 94
Mundaka Upanishad, 51, 85, 94

nirguna, 12, 14, 1, 5, 6, 7, 8, 15, 19, 20, 21, 22, 23, 29, 31, 32, 38, 40, 43, 44, 46, 47, 51, 62, 63, 64, 67, 74, 75, 88, 90, 91, 95, 100, 102
Nirgunan, 14
nirgunatvam, 28, 30, 46, 64, 65, 69, 87, 98, 100
nirvisesham, 30
nithya-suri, 37
No-Soul, 57
nyAsa, 14
Omar Khayyam, 98
paapa, 37
Paraashara Bhattar, 18, 19, 33, 67, 70, 75
param-jyoti, 42
patticcha-samuppaada, 57, 59
Peetaadhipathi, 35
pracchannna saugata, 51
prakata saugata, 51
prakruti, 10, 16, 17, 20, 22, 23, 24, 28, 34, 37, 38, 39, 40, 41, 42, 45, 47, 49, 56, 59, 60, 66, 70, 71, 72, 74, 76, 77, 79, 87
pramaana, 26, 28, 29, 30, 31, 41, 46
pratyaksham, 26, 30
prithvi, 36
psychosomatism, 78
punnya, 37
Raja Dharma, 46
rajas, 9, 16, 20, 22, 24, 28, 34, 37, 38, 71, 74
Ramanujacharya, 18, 85, 92, 100, 103, 104
S.M. Srinivasa Chari, 2, 104
saadhakaas, 8

saadhana, 8, 62
saakhaantara-adhikarana, 46
saamaanaadhi-karanya, 93
Sagunan, 14, 18
samasta-heya-pratyaneeka, 22, 40
samvaada, 15
sankalpa, 73, 75, 76, 78, 79
Sankara, 5, 20, 22, 40, 47, 51, 52, 53, 54, 56, 61, 65, 66, 74, 88, 89
Sankara Sahasranaama Bhaashya, 20
saranaagathi gadyam, 100
sarira-sariri-bhaavam, 72
Satadushani, 11, 12, 13, 1, 3, 34, 87, 90, 92, 99, 103, 104
sath, 16, 24, 42, 45, 47, 71, 91
sattva, 9, 16, 20, 22, 24, 28, 34, 37, 38, 39, 43, 70, 71, 74, 79
Sayana, 5
shlOkA, 10
shraddha, 13
siddha-traya, 51
smriti, 14, 2, 16, 28, 29, 31, 32, 33, 46, 62, 85
Soundaryalahari, 47
Sri Bhaashya, 1, 3, 85
Sri Krishna, 9, 10, 16, 17, 22, 39
Sri Mukkur Azhagiyasingar, 48
Sri Mukkur Lakshminarasimhacharia r, 3

Sri Ramanuja, 10, 1, 51, 83
Sri Rangam, 100
Sri Vaikuntam, 37, 38, 39
Sri Vedanta Desika, 1
Sri Vishnu Sahasranaama, 7, 14, 17, 18, 20, 31
sruta-prakaasika, 94
sruti, 14, 2, 26, 28, 29, 32, 33, 41, 42, 45, 46, 50, 68, 82, 83, 84, 85, 86, 88, 89, 91, 92
sruti vaakya, 28, 32, 33, 41, 42, 45, 46, 50, 85, 86, 91
stithi, 37, 77
suddha sattvam, 37
svaanubhava, 8
svarupa, 45, 94, 95, 96
svatah-siddham, 44
svayam prakaasam, 44
Svetasvataara, 7, 20, 82, 83
Swami Gambhirananda, 89
Swami Tapasyaananda, 20
Taittireeya Bhruguvalli, 41
Taittiriya Anandavalli, 6
Taittiriya Upanishad, 7, 44, 83, 93
tamas, 9, 16, 20, 22, 24, 28, 34, 37, 38, 71, 74
tapas, 13
tarka, 3, 30, 81
tattva, 10, 37, 42
tri-guNA, 9, 11
Tripitika-vaageeshwara-acharya, 56
ubhayalingatva sutra, 85
upaadaana-kaaranatvam, 72
upaasakaas, 8
upaaya, 61

upabrhmana, 29, 30, 31, 32, 33
upakramaadhi-karana-nyaaya, 90
Upanishads, 14, 4, 6, 7, 8, 15, 17, 18, 26, 41, 42, 43, 44, 54, 61, 63, 89, 93, 100
vaayu, 36
vAkyam, 13
veda shaakaa, 46
Vedaartha-Sangraha, 83
Vedanta, 11, 14, 1, 2, 3, 4, 5, 6, 16, 18, 20, 27, 29, 30, 31, 32, 33, 41, 42, 45, 48, 49, 51, 53, 54, 56, 62, 63, 64, 65, 66, 70, 73, 77, 79, 81, 82, 85, 86, 87, 88, 93, 97, 99, 100, 104, 111
Vedanta Sutra, 14, 86

Vedas, 7, 16, 17, 49, 54
Vignyaana-bhikshu, 52
visesha vibhuti, 31
Vishnu, 7, 12, 14, 16, 17, 18, 19, 20, 24, 27, 28, 29, 30, 31, 32, 38, 44, 52, 54, 61, 67, 74, 76, 86, 104
Visishtaadvaita, 14, 1, 2, 4, 7, 8, 16, 17, 18, 29, 41, 43, 45, 54, 63, 69, 70, 76, 77, 78, 81, 87, 94, 97, 98, 99, 104
volitional action, 59
vyaakarana, 3, 5, 30, 95
Walpola Rahula, 56, 60, 104
Yaamunaachaarya, 92
Yaamunachaarya, 51
yagnya, 13
yajantE, 13

www.ingramcontent.com/pod-product-compliance
Lightning Source LLC
LaVergne TN
LVHW061630070526
838199LV00071B/6635